THE METAPHYSICS OF
WILLIAM JAMES AND JOHN DEWEY

The METAPHYSICS of
WILLIAM JAMES and JOHN DEWEY

PROCESS AND STRUCTURE IN
PHILOSOPHY AND RELIGION

Thomas R. Martland, Jr.

GREENWOOD PRESS, PUBLISHERS
NEW YORK

Copyright © 1963 by Philosophical Library, Inc.

Reprinted by permission
of the Philosophical Library

First Greenwood Reprinting, 1969

PRINTED IN UNITED STATES OF AMERICA

I would like to take this opportunity to thank Professor Horace L. Friess of Columbia University for his friendship and advice in the preparation of this work. I would also like to express my appreciation to Professor John A. Hutchison, of Claremont Graduate School, and to Professor Daniel D. Williams of Union Theological Seminary for their help. Finally, I would like to acknowledge the great debt of inspiration I owe to my friend, Louise Allen Johnston. It is to her I dedicate this book.

TABLE OF CONTENTS

INTRODUCTION

This book aims to offer evidence for the thesis that in certain respects there is a congruence between philosophy and religion. This congruence should not be a complete surprise because both philosophy and religion as general disciplines distinct from particular historical manifestations are concerned with relating all phases of experience. At least initially, they are both human attempts to understand the whole world in which we live.[1]

Chapter I presents some religious examples in which certain features appear that later chapters will show to be congruent to philosophy. This chapter includes ancient religions which provided a cradle for our Western civilization, Canaan, Greece, and Christianity. Whatever else we may say about their witness, these religions reveal a common polarity of process and structure. By means of the attributes of their gods, they reflect an orientation to changing life and its significance in the construction of the future, plus a seemingly conflicting orientation toward the direction of life and its measure and control of the changing process itself. The illustrations which the book presents show that this polarity is not identically the same in each case, but that within each particular cultural variation it does exist.

For instance, within the predominantly agricultural society of Canaan, a paramount concern of the people is the coming of the new rainy season and the birth of the new crop. In so far as this concern expresses itself in the people's attempt to affect the crop and in their acceptance of its coming and going as ultimately significant in the meaning of the world, we have an orientation which accepts changing life as significant in the construction of the future. Baal, the fertility god who brings the seasonal growth, is its religious symbol. The people believed that by allying themselves with Baal they and he could affect the world in which they lived.

The other pole is the one that expresses itself in the acceptance of the necessity for a structural measure which controls and directs the changing life process itself. Within the predominantly agricultural society of Canaan, the people express this awareness in a concern for the regulation of the seasons and an acceptance of measure as of ultimate significance. El, the chief god of the pantheon, to whom all the gods must do homage even if only to fulfill their seasonal chores, is its religious symbol. In this case the people bow to the ordered world in which they live and acknowledge El as the overarching director of the processes of this world. Baal and El fulfill the needs that stem from basic patterns of mental behavior, from basic orientations that incline the people either to the process pole or the structural pole.

In the varied activities of the Greek city state there is an entirely different emphasis; and naturally this affects the character of the symbols fulfilling the two needs stemming from the patterns of mental behavior. A paramount concern of the Greeks was to find the laws governing their everyday activities and to direct these activities accordingly. A symbol of that stability beyond change is Apollo. He is akin to El, the organizer of the flow of seasons. It is to Apollo the lawgiver that society goes for directions on good government. However, the Greeks were also aware of the possibility that the changing life situations could extend beyond their measured order. Dionysus is a major symbol of this awareness. Fundamentally he is related to Baal but the process or acceptance of life which he symbolizes is not the optimistic one of bringing new seasonal crops, but contains an awareness of the tragic destructive side of ongoing life. Time and process bring new birth, but they also bring death and decay. Dionysus expresses the same human need for meaningfulness in the changing life situation; but in their cultural situation, the Greeks saw him as largely representing an awareness of the dark side of that meaningfulness.

The cultural concern found in early Christianity also has left its mark on the expression of these two patterns of mental behavior. The social concern in the Christian community does not center itself on adhering to the transcendent laws governing change as it did in Greece, but is in some ways more akin to the Canaanite optimistic interest in the changes to come. The Christian looked for redemption from the sinful state in which he found himself. He was concerned with salvation. Therefore he turned his attention to the symbol representing the meaningfulness of time and process; he turned his attention to that which would free him from the being of what is, and would open up for him the possibilities inherent in the becoming of time. Jesus Christ, God the Son, fulfills this need while God the Father represents the other need, the need for a transcendent judge acknowledging the rules of the status quo, or the sinful state as it is without the Son.[2] There is another interesting similarity between the Canaanite Ugaritic myth and Christianity. Just as El is in his way the bringer of the organized flow of seasons, thereby the bringer of Baal, so God the Father is, in his way, the bringer of redemption and salvation. He has allowed His Son to die for mankind.

The philosophical material which this book presents in order to show the congruence of philosophy and religion is that literature critical of pragmatic naturalism in America from approximately 1900 to 1950 and pragmatic naturalism itself as represented by William James and John Dewey. I chose this material because of its extreme difference from the religions Chapter I discusses. Pragmatic naturalism's alleged separation from any specific religion made its use a more crucial test of the thesis that religion and philosophy have a congruence, than would, say, Hellenistic philosophy which operates in the same cultural milieu as that of the religions studied.

Chapter II is specifically concerned with the criticism of pragmatic naturalism. Whatever else we may say about it, this discussion, to the extent that it centered upon pragmatic naturalism and expressed itself as a critical evaluation of that philosophical way of looking at the world, also revealed a polarity of process and structure. To the extent that each contributor was critical of pragmatic naturalism, he understood that philosophy to be a methodological "tough-minded" attempt to find an ultimately significant place in the world for aspiring desire, change and satisfaction. The critics interpreted pragmatic naturalism as an attempt to assert the validity of process. Therefore, to the extent that each contributor was a critic of pragmatic naturalism, every positive contribution to the discussion centered on the need for structure, measure or form, to give the process its meaning and direction. Whether it is just to pragmatic naturalism or not, the critical discussion reduced itself, first, to an understanding of that philosophy as expressing only an orientation to changing life and its significance in the construction of the future, and secondly, to an assertion of the validity of the other orientation, the orientation concerned with the direction of the changing life process itself by measure and order.

In a sense Chapters III and IV are supplementary, because to some extent Chapters I and II already establish the congruence of philosophy and religion. Both Chapter I, dealing with religion, and Chapter II, dealing with philosophy, reveal a similar polarity of process and structure. However, both chapters have left unsettled problems. In the examination of religion it seems that each particular cultural expression carried its polarity a step further than the mere recognition of the two orientations or patterns of mental behavior. Each religious expression found room for acceptance of the two needs. The final witness of Chapter I is a co-acceptance of these needs. El builds Baal a temple; the Greek people worship both Apollo and Dionysus at Delphi; the Christians invoke God the Father and God the Son in the same prayer. Therefore the question which naturally arises from Chapter I is: Is this co-acceptance also an aspect of the congruence between philosophy and religion? Does philosophy as well as religion end in such co-acceptance?

The second problem arises from the philosophical discussion in Chapter II. This problem might be more serious. An imaginary critic of the thesis that there is a congruence between philosophy and religion could say, "All right, it is true that religion expresses the two poles, but your choice of a critical debate over a philosophy held to represent one exclusive pole as the philosophical witness to that same polarity is unfair. For the presentation of a philosophy stressing *one* pole will necessarily encourage a critical emphasis on the need for the other pole. If pragmatic naturalism is only wedded to process, it becomes an artificial set-up that by its biased nature forces critical debate to speak in terms of that bias and the necessary corollary, i.e., process and structure. Pragmatic naturalism's process orientation, as the critical discussion revealed it, weakens its effectiveness as an example of the congruence of philosophy and religion."

In order to answer both of these problems, Chapter III presents a detailed examination of William James' philosophy and Chapter IV presents that of John Dewey's. These chapters aim to prove that James and Dewey *are* well aware of both patterns of mental behavior, and that they *do* find a place within their empirical philosophy not only for the associated "toughminded" characteristics of aspiring desire, change and satisfaction, but also for those associated "tenderminded" characteristics of stability, limitation, and control. These chapters point out that experience tells them that nature not only is open to our desires and our needs, in fact is incomplete without them, but that it also presents obstacles and conditions to the fulfilling of our desires. In other words, Nature has a character of its own. It has, as James said, "inner relations [that] . . . our thought . . . must eternally take [into] account." It has within itself, as Dewey said, "what in the literal sense must be called ends, terminals, arrests, enclosures." These assertions declare nature's structure. Whether their particular declaration of the place of structure in the ultimate picture of things is satisfactory or not is not at issue. What is important is that pragmatic naturalism transcends its emphatic process orientation and thinks also in terms of order and direction. Thus, Chapters III and IV solve both unsettled problems. First, the thought of James and Dewey is evidence that the congruence of philosophy and religion can extend to a co-acceptance of process and structure. Second, this assertion of co-acceptance also reaffirms the value of the critical discussion of pragmatic naturalism in asserting the congruence between religion and philosophy. As individual worshippers had the opportunity in Canaan and Greece to relate themselves to Baal and El, Dionysus and Apollo, so the philosophers concerned with pragmatic naturalism in America had the opportunity to relate themselves to process and structure.

Chapter I

PROCESS AND STRUCTURE AS SYMBOLIZED IN THREE ANCIENT RELIGIONS

A comparison of reactions to John Dewey's philosophical sentence "The knowledge of what is possible is the beginning of happiness" with reactions to the religious question "Is it possible to emulate the divine?" may make clearer the congruence between philosophy and religion that this book attempts to indicate. The comparison is effective because each sentence insists on an interpretation of the nature of what is ultimately significant in the universe before any further speculation is possible. Before the philosophical sentence can be discussed at any length, an interpretation of "what is possible" (at least implicitly) is necessary. Before the religious question can be discussed, an interpretation of the nature of the divine is necessary.

Dewey himself asserted as much in his article "Classicism as an Evangel" when he traced back the two possible reactions to his sentence.[1] According to him, the first reaction is to think in terms of human possibilities and to derive the lesson of limitation and check upon aspiration and desire. If man would only know his own limits or his own possibilities, he would obtain happiness. He would not ask for more than his due. Such a viewpoint assumes that the world is by its very nature structured. It establishes limits to the restless flow of life. Measure, order, proportion and limit reveal its ultimate character. Reason is the voluntary perception and intellectual adoption of this structure or

1

measure as the rule of life. The other reaction to the sentence is to think in terms of the possibilities of things and to consider the world as open to change and transformation. If man would only concentrate on changing the world he could obtain his happiness. The world would be his instrument to happiness. Such a viewpoint assumes that the world by its very nature is changing and flowing. It stands open to our suggestions because these suggestions, as well as our hopes and desires, are part of its process and can affect its flow. Nature is uncertain and reason is the voluntary instrument to be applied to it so as to direct its flow toward the hoped for re-creation leading to happiness. To apply reason in this dynamic sense is the rule of life.

Elsewhere Dewey carries his analysis further and comes to the conclusion that the two types of personality which these reactions reveal differ at root in the extent that they allow the craving for the fixed and sure to dominate. This craving is in all of us, but when it rules we hypostatize our present discriminations into ultimate laws which transcend the uncertainties of everyday happenings. In effect, it means the retreat into the certain, the traditional and the accepted. This is equivalent to looking at nature's structure in order to obtain happiness. When we refuse to allow the craving for the fixed and the certain to dominate, we unite our philosophy with life. There is no ultimate law transcending the present uncertainties, so we must courageously face the open universe with its plural and unfinished directions, its hazards, its novelties and its unadjusted cross-currents. This is equivalent to looking at nature's flowing possibilities in order to obtain happiness.

Sometime earlier William James had made a similar distinction in terms of "tender mindedness" and "tough mindedness." He associated rationalism (going by 'principles'), intellectualism, idealism, optimism, religion, free will, monism, and dogmatism with the former, and empiricism (going by 'facts'), sensationalism, materialism, pessimism, irreligion, fatalism, pluralism, and skepticism with the latter.[2] Although these associations may cloud Dewey's sharp dichotomy, it is evident from this listing, and elsewhere, that James was using the same distinguishing marks to describe different types of people as Dewey does. He was distinguishing those people who live by principles or ideals from those people who live by the crude facts of life. He wanted to distinguish those people who live by eternal rules that direct life from those people who let life direct life. He wanted to distinguish those people who say no to the pulsating changes of concrete living by denying that they have ultimate significance from those people who say yes and accept these as of ultimate value in understanding the universe.

If we apply this same sort of speculation to the religious question "Is it possible to emulate the divine?" the same sort of dichotomy is in evidence. Again the first possible type of reaction is to think in terms of limitation and check upon aspiration and desire. Man must know his limits. It is not for him to equal the gods. The gods are of such a nature as to stand apart from man, and they insist upon his recognition of the limits beyond which he cannot go. Man cannot emulate the divine. Such a viewpoint assumes that the world is a structural whole in which each segment fits in place. Measure, order, proportion, and limit are its ultimate characteristics. Reason is the voluntary perception and intellectual adoption of this structure or measure as the rule of life. The other possible reaction to the question is to think in terms of open possibilities and human potentiality. The gods are of such a nature as to involve themselves with man and this relates him to the powers of the universe. Man can emulate the divine. The gods listen to his prayers and respond to his needs. Such a viewpoint assumes that the changeable and flowing world is significant and reponsive to man's power. Reason is the voluntary instrument he

3

applies to accomplish the hoped for result. The rule of life is to live so as to be in touch with the divine, with the powers of the world.

Up to this point, at least, it seems philosophy and religion are related in so far as they attempt to express themselves on the basis of root interpretations of what is ultimately significant in the universe. To this extent both disciplines stem from an interpretation of the universe that rests in turn upon a personality that needs to so interpret the universe. Philosophical interpretations of the nature of the universe and religious interpretations of the nature of God are answers to the needs stemming from the same types of personality. For each basic type of personality there is a corresponding god and a corresponding interpretation of what is Real. These types of personality create the art products of philosophy and religion. Man finds the Real for which he looks. Man finds the Divine for whom he looks. Saying the same thing but switching the field of action, the Real, or the Divine, presents itself to a particular person as that person is prepared to meet it, or him.

CANAANITE RELIGION

Historically, the most obvious religious expression of these two needs is the Greek Apollo and Dionysus. Apollo represents the satisfaction of the need stemming from the type of personality that looks to a universe of structure, whereas Dionysus symbolizes the satisfaction of the need stemming from the type of personality that looks to a universe in process. Thus, Morris Cohen uses these religious deities when he tries to express his philosophical principle of polarity in terms of religious symbol. His philosophical principle is that "whatever the future may bring, it is clear that any attempt to see the limitation of the characteristically modern emphasis on the 'dynamic,' the 'evolutionary,' and

4

'progressive,' must pay greater attention to the principle of polarity as the union of the values of order and stability with the values of change and progress." [3] He translates this philosophical principle concerning the values of order and stability, and the values of change and progress, into religious terms with the following: "The romantic effort to enthrone Dionysus and the chthonic deities has always proved worse than sterile when it has meant the banishing of the Olympic gods of the air and the light. Inspiration or Dionysiac frenzy is barren or destructive except when it submits to rational labour. For not all who rave are divinely inspired." [4] Note the clue Cohen gives to his own particular understanding of which pole is the more significant.

Another example of the tendency to express oneself in terms of the Greek deities is Charles Morris. In his *Paths of Life* he considers many different religious characters, but when he calls attention to their attribute of loyalty to restrictive laws or to creative life he employs the Greek deities as the over-arching symbol "The Christians, Buddhists, and Apollonians agree in one feature: they are all restrainers of the Dionysian impulses within the limits of a socially approved morality; in contrast, the Dionysians, the Prometheans, and the Mohammedans are releasers of impulses which threaten to upset the institutions of established society." [5] Other examples of this awareness of religious polarity in Greek terms surely are not hard to find. For instance, note the following:

Augustinianism emerges, not as a conglomerate of indiscriminate borrowings, but as a mature philosophy which seeks to do justice to all aspects of experience and in particular to overcome the apparent discrepancy between the demands of order and those of process, i.e., between so called Apolline and Dionysiac elements in life.[6]

5

The probable advantage of using the Greek deities Dionysus and Apollo as the representative symbols of these two forces in life is that they represent more completely detailed pictures of the developed forces than other known polytheistic religions. An example of what I mean by this will become clear if we compare the developed features of the Greek deities with the Canaanite deities of approximately the fourteenth century B.C. The later and more clearly defined Greek expressions bring out not only the existence of the classical or structural emphasis and the instrumentalistic or dynamic emphasis, but also offer a rich source for the analysis of the religious implications which arise when you examine these two conflicting types of personality. These implications are generally missing from the Canaanite myths, but it is important to remember that the Greek religion depicts a society which existed perhaps six centuries later than that of the Canaanites.[7]

My source of information for the Canaanite religion is H. L. Ginsberg's translation of the "Ugaritic Myths, Epics and Legends" published in *Ancient Near Eastern Texts*.[8] However, I must admit that my interpretation of these Ras Shamra texts discovered in 1928 is largely my own. Because of the recent date of discovery, scholars are still analyzing these texts and are just now coming to general conclusions about the character of the types of superhuman beings described. See, for example, Marvin Pope, *El in the Ugaritic Texts*.[9] But my general hypothesis is not completely personal. I owe a great deal to Professor Theodore H. Gaster's treatment of "The Religion of the Canaanites," in *Forgotten Religions*,[10] especially pages 118 through 121. In this analysis he points to the "punctual" and the "durative" levels of the Canaanite religion, levels which, incidentally, he believes exist in all primitive religions. He asserts "all that obtains in the immediate here and now is but the punctual realization of something which is in essence durative and sempiternal." By this he means that the activities

6

of primitive society are effective in so far as they are the immediate here and now expression of an action which is being done *eo ipso* on a permanent "ideal" level. For instance, the actions of the human king have validity in so far as they are in tune with the actions of the local god or gods. The former is, so to speak, the punctual immanent expression of that which is valid on the "ideal" transcendent durative level.

My point is to take these transcendent and immanent levels, which Gaster clearly depicts, and associate them with El, who is "essentially a transcendent being," and Baal, whose nature is "necessarily immanent." Now, I would like to make clear the conflicting nature of the two levels, but I also hope to make it clear later that I agree with Gaster when he claims that within the Canaanite religion it is the function of the immanent level to express the transcendent. In effect this is asserting that within the Canaanite religion there is a priority of the transcendent. This becomes apparent symbolically when Baal, previously the Son of Dagon, becomes the Son of El. This new mythical harmony implies priority but it does not imply willing obedience or tractability on the part of the son. The myth stories themselves are a witness to this fact.

El

The Canaanite myth of Baal and El centers around the attempts of one of the Ugaritic Gods, Baal, to establish himself as God of the Earth. His opposition outwardly consists of Yam, the God of the Sea, and Mot, the God of Death and Sterility; but fundamentally, the real problem lies with El, the chief god of the pantheon. In the battle for power and establishment that develops, the Canaanites symbolically depict the mutually exclusive nature of the two concepts of the divine, and of the types of personality or mental make-up that pledge adherence to one deity rather than the other. By picturing these natures as mutually exclusive they also emphasize the idea that a swallowing up of one need by the other would be impossible. Their solution to the struggle, like the solution to the struggle depicted in the Greek tradition, is one of co-existence. In practical terms this is an expression of the need for both the structural and the dynamic principles of life.

The conflict between Baal and El immediately becomes evident when "El the King," [11] "The Father of Man," [12] turns to support Yam against Baal. When Baal successfully eliminates Yam, El then turns to support Mot.[13] Despite this hostility of El's, Baal dares not be angry with him, for the gods are afraid of the power of El.[14] It is to El that all gods must go if they are discontented; it is to El that they must go if they want special favors; [15] it is into El's field that they must enter, prostrating themselves before him, "doing him homage," [16] if they want his permission even for what is their due.[17] Anger at El, in such a situation, would simply mean a sure rejection of special favors such as Baal's request for a temple built in his honor. In fact, El originally rejected this request; and Baal was forced to enlist the aid of other gods to intercede for him.[18] The same relationship that exists between El and the other gods is valid for El and Man, except that man is another step removed. El may grant men their wishes, but they must find another god to intercede to El for them.[19]

In a not too detailed picture we see that El is essentially a god separated from man's world, and the supreme god of the pantheon. The gods may approach him directly but man can only approach him indirectly, through the intercession of one of the lesser gods. Both gods and men are directed to offer him their sacrifices [20] (even El's wife, the "progenitress of the gods" [21] must propitiate Bull El Benign, must do "obeisance to the Creator of Creatures;" [22]), and both receive favors and rights—Baal, the immortal, a temple; [23] Daniel, the mortal, a son.[24]

In direct opposition to El, not only in action, but in principle, is Baal, the "Rider of the Clouds," [25] "Prince Lord of Earth." [26] Fundamentally Baal is a rain and fertility god. This is evident in the story of his struggle to assert himself over the might of El's favorites. After he has gained the initial victory he is somehow led into the power of Mot, and Mot kills him (Mot's very name means death).[27] He is the god of all that lacks life and vitality. When this happens "parch'd is the furrow of soil. . . . Parched is El's soil's furrow: Baal neglects the furrow of his tillage." [28] This happens because the earth is Baal's dominion,[29] and it is he who opens rifts in the clouds [30] to allow rain and dew.[31] When at last Baal's virgin sister, Anath, avenges his murder, dissects his body and plants it in the ground, he again comes to life and "the heaven fat did rain, the wadies flow with honey." [32] In all probability, then, this story of Baal was a "seasonal myth based on the traditional ritual drama of the autumn festival." [33] For the people, its depiction was a meaningful procedure to effect Baal's powers by so-called "rites of impulsion." [34] The success of the rites brought about the proper success of the seasons and the presence of Baal as that indwelling dynamic force activating the organic process.[35] During these rites he became the head of the worshipping group and the source of all of its gifts.[36] As the indwelling dynamic force he stimulated his votaries to such an extent that they "cut themselves after their custom with swords and lances until the blood gushed out upon them." [37]

These rites in which Baal as a fertility god demands his votaries to effect his gifts of rain and growth subconsciously express the idea of a mutual relationship between the deity and man. The possession of the votaries by the presence of the deity is also evident in the procedure of the called for rites. This possession leads to enthusiasm and excess. Baal, who possesses his votaries and brings rain for his people, represents the deity who appeals to the personality that is concerned with man's relatedness to the powers of creation and accepts nature's open possibilities. Man's actions and enthusiasms do have ultimate significance. The world is changed because of them. Comparing this position with that of El's is like comparing a God who is a personal individual experience to one who is a public institution. With El, the personal relationship is one of subservience and hoped for communication; with Baal it is one of kinship and possible communion.[38] He symbolically represents the limiting principle of man's aspirations. When the mortal Daniel wants a favor from the divine powers, he goes to Baal, who understands man's plight and cares for him, but he, Baal, in turn must go to El, the establisher of limits and laws.[39] In this sense El is transcendent. Baal the symbol of man's possibilities of creation, of possibility, is immanent. This means that powers of creation are really with man and that he can change the world. Religiously this idea is expressed when man believes God cares for him and protects him. That my personal efforts are meaningful means God, the religious expression of the ultimate, considers me and them to be important.[40] El was well aware of Baal's care for the people when he cried out upon hearing of Baal's death: "Baal's dead;—What becomes of the people. Dagon's son—What of the masses. 'After Baal I'll descend into earth." [41] In other words, Baal is related to the need for believing that life is significant, that re-creation is possible, that man may emulate the divine. El is related to the need for believing that life has a transcendent principle, at which man must aim; that beyond the changes of everyday happenings there is a stable meaningful structure that directs and controls. Baal is related to active doing. El is related to the law and order of doing.

It is interesting to note the mythical priority revealed in the Canaanite struggle between El and Baal. The burden of establishing validity lies with the dynamic creative pole against the already established pole of limitation and measure. This seems to be the nature of the case. Re-creation and enthusiasm have no initial place in the status quo, in the established order. The confusion about Baal's background mythically expresses this struggle of the dynamic for acceptance by the static. In some passages he is directly referred to as the son of Dagon,[42] yet elsewhere Anath is mentioned as his sister, and she most definitely is considered to be a child of El's.[43] The implication is that originally Baal was not a member of the Ugaritic pantheon, but due to the popular acceptance the people began to think of him as one of the gods. When this happened he merited the honor of being a child of El, symbolically expressing the acceptance within the ultimate explanation of things of the human need to feel that life is meaningful.

When we consider the complete Baal-El relationship, it seems evident that Baal's popularity was the prime motivating force behind his final acceptance as a member of the Ugaritic pantheon. Not only is active resistance evident from El in his treatment of Baal's request for a temple, but also there is evidence of insubordination, conspiracy and connivance against El on the part of Baal and his allies. An example of conspiracy, for instance, is Baal's use of the divine bludgeons Yagrush and Ayamur to smite El's favorite, Yam. These bludgeons were gifts of the divine artisan Kothar whom El originally instructed to build a palace for Yam.[44] This certainly represents a revolt of some consequence against the official pattern.

Co-acceptance

Finally, though, despite all these connivances, the inherent opposition between El and Baal results in acceptance. The symbol representing the need for order and limit accepts the symbol representing the need for open possibilities

11

and active creation. The Canaanite myth finds ultimate room for both symbols, expressing a more complete understanding of man's needs. El establishes Baal in his rightful place among the gods; he is accepted as a proper god of the pantheon, receives strong allies, and eventually gets his much deserved palace of gold and silver.[45] Above all else, El personally accepts him, henceforth living side by side with him. When "Kindly El Benign" hears of the death of "Puissant Baal," he

> sits on the ground;
> Pours dust of mourning on his head,
>> Earth of mortification on his pate;
>> And puts on sackcloth and loincloth.
> He cuts a gash with a stone,
>> Incisions with . . .
> He gashes his cheeks and his chin,
>> He harrows the roll of his arm.
> He plows his chest like a garden,
>> Harrows his back like a plain.
> He lifts up his voice and cries:
> "Baal's dead!—What becomes of the people?" [46]

The effect of this establishment is immediately evident in the popular mind. In practical religion, Asherah, the consort of El, the progenitress of the gods, becomes the consort of Baal [47] and the people give Baal the main temple at Ugarit.[48] Finally, if the Israelite Old Testament can be taken as evidence, by the middle of the eighth century B.C., devotion to Baal dominated the land of Canaan.[49] El is still supreme but the people belong to Baal.

Greek Religion

Along with some important additions, the Greek religious scene from approximately the seventh century B.C. to

12

the fourth century B.C. reveals the same basic polarity as does the religious scene of the Canaanites. The logical implications of each need have here had time to develop, and so in one sense the poles stand in sharper outline, but in another sense the need for both poles is anticipated. This results in each pole being associated with or itself employing elements more logically associated with the other pole.

In a general way, the Homeric Olympian Gods and the chthonian cult of the Eleusinian mysteries, which official Athenian sentiment modified, represent the Classical Greek religious expressions of the two types of personality. The Homeric gods, including Zeus and his entourage, represent a religious expression of the "rational" need for moderation and limit, while the Eleusinian mysteries, associated primarily with Demeter, the mother of life, and her associates represent a religious expression of the "impulsive" need for creative activity. The first is a religious expression of the need for fixed ends, with devotion to lawful tradition and certainty. The second is a religious expression of the need for meaningful vitality, attached to more elemental matters in experience and change. These two religious approaches are sometimes labelled Olympian and Chthonian, to stand respectively for the cults of the pure air about the tops of the sacred mountains and for cults of the earth and the regions beneath it. Notice that the two concepts even take their logical geographical location. The symbol representing the need for law and order and devotion to "principles" is located about the tops of the sacred mountains. The symbol representing the need for enthusiasm, and devotion to "facts of life," is located in the regions beneath the earth.

At times the Olympian and Chthonian implications tend to fuse; for instance the transcendent gods of the structural order allowed a mortal man to become immortal, thereby confusing the static order of things.[50] But it is true that this confusion of implications is relatively rare in classical times.

13

The deities kept their character and the Greek heeded Plato's command that the people "shall not confuse the infernal deities and their rites with the Gods who are termed heavenly and their rites." [51] Religion maintained the correct distinctions and the two sets of gods stand for concepts clear and pure—the Olympians standing for the limitation of man; the Chthonians standing for the unlimited possibilities of men. Is it possible to emulate the gods? The Olympians would say no. The Chthonians, yes.

Apollo

The religion dedicated to the Homeric Olympian gods "seems to have lacked completely, or almost completely, the passionate self-scrutiny, the yearning for intimate personal communication with the god, and the striving for mystic extinction of the personal ego in the deity." [52] It was a religion that was thoroughly concerned with the prevention of the sin of *hybris*. Man must keep his distance and not aspire to higher spheres. The gods go one way, man the other, and the two are essentially different. The Greek connected *hybris*, which means haughtiness in word and deed, presumption, presumptuous conduct or simply pride, with the Homeric phrase, "beyond the alloted portion." [53] It is the desire to be like god, to reach beyond man's mortal portion, and this desire inevitably leads to destruction, "for the god suffers pride in none but himself." [54] *Ate* was the term the Greek used to describe the condition that made one desire to be like the gods. It meant infatuation or moral blindness. The term also includes the ruin that results.[55] The Greek believed that moral blindness, or *ate*, especially afflicted men of high station whose exceptional prosperity lifted them too near the felicity that is the possession of the Olympian gods. "There was no mortal, nor ever would be, to whom at birth some admixture of misfortune was not allotted; the greater the man, the greater the misfortune." [56] If man forgot this fact, *ate* possessed him. It is this that Homer warns against when Odysseus visits Hades and witnesses the eternal sufferings of three great sinners: Tityus, Tantalus, and Sisyphus, who were all guilty of overstepping their allotted portion.[57]

The sins of *hybris* and *ate* define the feeble state of man by negation, and also provide an interesting insight into the nature of the gods the Greeks worshipped. The doctrine of *hybris* reveals the jealousy of the Homeric gods. First it is abundantly clear that "such gods could have no thought of redeeming man from the world and raising him to themselves." [58] This is because the gods and man are separated. That which has the strongest impact of separation upon man is death, and it is death that puts the gulf between him and god. "If man is immortal, then he is god. This is universal in Greece." [59] Even man's hopeless wish to transcend his separation is enough to draw down the jealousy of heaven.

The great message of the Homeric gods then is "seek not to become a Zeus. If a share of these good things fall to thy lot, thou hast everything. Men must die, things that must die befit them." [60] In other words, the Greeks emphasized the structural universe, and the need for law and order, principles and moderation. Their cultural concern was to find the laws governing their everyday activities and to direct these activities accordingly. Within this social context their divine is that which stands for the fixed and established above the flux of nature. The command is to beware of *hybris*. Do not direct emphasis toward creativity and becoming so much as toward how creativity and becoming come about. Man is not to look toward life but toward the principles that control life.

The Greek carried his great concentration on transcendent principles, and on the separation between himself and god, one step further when he considered whether the gods will, or can, answer the prayers of devout men. In other words, the question was whether the deities can and will change the order and limitation placed on man. In order to find an answer the first thing the Greek had to decide was whether prayers ever reach the gods. To this first question Homer implies a yes. He asserts that the "very gods, for all their greater excellence and majesty and power are capable of being swayed." [61] However, whether this fact that the gods do hear pleas and are capable of being affected by them is of any worth is another question. The next question is, can the gods change man's limited place in the fixed order of things even if they have a mind to do so? In some cases it didn't seem to be so. "The Son of Cronos of the crooked ways saw what was happening and was distressed. He sighed, and said to Hera his Sister and Wife: 'Fate is unkind to me—Sarpedon, whom I deeply love is destined to be killed by Patroclus.' " [62] In this reference it is clear that even Zeus must submit to the all powerful law. Plato substantiates this when he says "even God is said not to be able to fight against necessity." [63] If this is the last word we already see that prayers are useless. The gods may hear and be swayed but they are helpless. But this is not the last word. In distinction to the above, Homer has Princess Nausicaa say to Odysseus: "As for these ordeals of yours, they must have been sent you by Olympian Zeus, who follows his will in dispensing happiness to people whatever their merits. You have no choice but to endure." [64] In support, Hesiod says: "There is no way to escape the will of Zeus." [65] Perhaps Aeschylus resolves the contradictions between these views and the one above when he says that the "all-seeing Zeus and Fate come down" in agreement.[66] Suppose Aeschylus is correct and we ignore or deny the helplessness of the gods, and suppose the other requirements necessary for a hearing from the gods are present: (1) man humbly acknowledges his inferiority to the gods and is free from *ate;* (2) he is capable of swaying the gods; and (3) the gods can do something about it; even then, can we assert that they will be

16

swayed and therefore will do something? Apollo provides the truly consistent, rational and Greek answer. To Poseidon the Earth-Shaker's challenge to a fight in defense of the Trojans, he answers: "Lord of the Earthquake . . . you would credit me with very little sense if I fought you for the sake of men, those wretched creatures who, like the leaves, flourish for a little while on the bounty of the earth and flaunt their brilliance, but in a moment droop and fade away." [67]

This answer is fully consistent with the concept of deity that says no to man's ultimate aspirations and with the concept of philosophy that looks to ultimate laws that regulate and limit possibilities. It is interesting to note that it came from Apollo, the god who exerted the greatest influence upon the religious life of Greece. It was he whom ancient art represents more frequently than any other deity.[68] If the Olympian religion stands for anything at all, "it is Apollo whose form most clearly manifests it." [69] "He is the very embodiment of the Hellenic spirit. Everything that marks off the Greek outlook from that of other peoples . . . beauty of every sort, whether of art, music, poetry of youth, sanity and moderation—all are summed up in Apollo." [70] He represents the concept of the transcendent deity beyond man's emulation, above all others. Though he was only supposed to proclaim the thoughts of the highest god of heaven and not be that god himself, the people accepted his proclamations as infallibly from that highest god.[71] If we are to know of the Olympian gods, we must go to their leading spokesman. Apollo spoke for Zeus and his counsel was Zeus' counsel.

The precepts inscribed on the fabric of his temple at Delphi clearly reveal a nature devoted to limitation, order and measure. Some of them are: Curb thy spirit, Observe the limit, Hate *hybris*, Keep a reverent tongue, Fear authority, Bow before the divine, Glory not in strength, Keep women under rule.[72] These commands are a perfect summary

17

in personal terms of the attitudes a man must have in a world ruled by eternal order. Their keynote is a demand for limitation and restraint, coupled with a recognition of man's distance from those principles. The stress is on the knowledge of what man is, and how great the interval is which separates him from the greatness of the eternal gods. Socrates' foil, Critias, refers to the familiar Delphic motto "know thyself," and says that " 'know thyself' and 'Be temperate' are the same." [73] This is exactly correct. Apollo exacts measure from his disciples and to this end he requires self knowledge. This is thinking in terms of the limits of human possibilities, and the automatic effect is to focus attention on the contrast between man and the ultimate eternal principles of life. This leads to temperance. There is also the implication that in order to know your own measure you must prevent pride and excess, for they interfere with the sharp lines of individuality. To measure is to set boundaries. Thus Apollo becomes "the god of individuation, the god who sets the boundaries of justice."

But temple precepts are not the only key to his nature. Symbolically the Greek always associated Apollo with music and the bow.[74] Otto claims this heightens the emphasis on the characteristics of distance and clarity. In reference to the musical trait he says: "The song of the most alert of all the gods does not arise dreamlike out of an intoxicated soul but flies directly towards a clearly seen goal, the truth and the rightness of its aim is a sign of its divinity." In reference to the bow he asks: "Is not the bow a symbol of distance? The arrow is sped from a place unseen and flies to its mark from afar." [75] The Greeks also associated Apollo with law and order. This was his most important and influential aspect. Not only did the Greeks go to Apollo at Delphi for the ordering of "the institution of temples and sacrifices, and the entire services of gods, demigods, and heroes; also the ordering of the repositories of the dead," [76] but almost all peoples went to Delphi with all sorts of con-

18

cerns. Herodotus reports, for instance, that "the Cyrenaeans, in their affliction, sent to Delphi to enquire what ordering of their state should best give them prosperity." [77] It is these Apolline interests which are more obviously related to the transcendent characteristics of ultimate limitation and moderation and they were Apollo's concern throughout his religious reign. They were his when later he lived side by side with Dionysus, from roughly the sixth to the fourth century B.C., and they were his already in the pages of the *Iliad* and the *Odyssey*.[78]

It is interesting to note that it was through this function of lawgiver, which is fundamentally an expression of concern for established cultural forms, that Apollo revealed his receptivity toward a personal concern for the people, symbolically representing the other need, a concern for the place of human creativity and change in the total picture of things. Once he assumed the habitat of Delphi he had no choice. The people consulted his oracle and somehow or other he had to answer. The Greeks wanted divine guidance on how to avoid misfortune in the future. They wanted certainty. This was in character, but their assumption that the gods would provide the guidance was not. The Greeks asked for a prophetic insight into the future, and by so doing, they asked Apollo to fulfill the other need, the need to feel a relatedness to the divine. Prophecy of its very nature compromises the Apollo that thought it senseless to fight over wretched men. It compromises the fixed and sharp individuality of man and god, and it compromises the command to "observe the limit." Its existence assumes a connection between god and man. I am speaking here not only of the special expression of prophecy that "cleaves to all frenzy," as Euripides described it in the *Bacchae*, but of all prophecy, of the basic implication behind the very attempt to ask a deity to advise a human being. Not only does prophecy compromise the sharp clear individuality and separation but there is the implication that Apollo wants it that way. The implication is that Apollo cares for man; that man, with Apollo's help, can really avoid misfortune, can really transcend his fate, can really change the world, can really make it new.[79] Whenever the Greek examined the gall bladder or the liver of the sacrifice, listened to the note of a bird, stood by an altar, or watched a flight of birds, he was irrationally attempting to make contact with the immortals and thereby in some way influence his tomorrow. The implication is that the order of things is open and uncertain. Man can change it and direct it if he knows for what to look.

Apollo's first mythical contact with Delphi emphasizes this confrontation of transcendency with immanency, of static, structural principles and open, flowing process. When he first came to Delphi, "where Themis at that time used to deliver oracles," he was forced to kill the guardian snake Python which attempted to hinder him from approaching.[80] Note that Apollo came to Delphi; Delphi was not his in the beginning. Also, the snake Python resisted his arrival. Originally Apollo was without the oracle and without the immanent implications of prophecy, and by meriting resistance from the original powers of the Oracle, the myth implies that he brought something to the oracle. He is therefore Apollo plus the oracle. In other words, he is at Delphi, a transcendent god, the god standing for the separation of man and God using immanent means, making contact with man. All of his actions at Delphi, his ecstatic prophetess used to administer the oracle, his introduction of Dionysus to Athens, his support of hero worship, are simply expressions of means. Apollo uses the means to serve his purposes, but it is Apollo that stands and uses Delphi. He is not Delphi. He is the god at Delphi. Symbolically this means that the dynamic need of prophecy has not forced the compromising of the structural need which Apollo represents. It means that structure can use creativity and enthusiasm but that it must preserve its form, its limit.

The god that finally shared Delphi with Apollo was Dionysus. The cult of this divinity is different in every particular from anything that resembles the Homeric concept of Greek worship of the gods. Apollo is the god of light, of clarity, of ethical moderation. He stresses freedom from wild emotions, measured restraint, self-knowledge, philosophical calm. His preference is for stability rather than change, for being rather than becoming, moderation in feelings, the specific, the well-formed, the finite, the clear, the harmonious. He represents the forces of stability and the ordered formal principles which control change. He tends to be the symbol for the hypostatization of the fixed and essential ways found to be successful in the past. In this sense he is the symbol for the truths of today and his precepts stifle the attempts to group anew. He is the symbol for all rational transcendent principles or laws that are considered to be necessary to direct the flux. He is the symbol of that which his supporters insist all religions must acknowledge. As Morris Cohen says, "No genuine religion is possible for the great mass of humanity except as it stimulates and is in turn fed by the sense of transcendance of something greater than our petty selves and beyond that which we can grasp immediately." [81]

Dionysus is the symbol of the attempt to seek relief from the burden of the social and self-controlled through man's desire to abandon himself to the need of enthusiasm and impulsive activity. He stands for an attachment to life rather than to principle or laws. Nietzsche says he represents a "yea saying to life, even to its strongest and most difficult problems: the will to life rejoicing at its own inexhaustibleness in the sacrifice of its highest types—this is what I called Dionysian." [82] Worship of Dionysus reaffirms the union between man and nature. Man can emulate the gods. Where

Apollo observed and therefore was detached, Dionysus participates. The follower of Dionysus says yes to nature and takes part in its changes and its flux. He takes joy not in comprehending the eternal concept of being but has eternal joy in becoming and in change. If Apollo is concerned with establishing measure, individuality, and sharp clarity, Dionysus enjoys tearing the veil of Maya and seeing everything as the mysterious Primordial Unity or, in terms more familiar, seeing everything participating in everything else. The sharp lines of individuality are gone. Emphasis is on unlimited possibilities and determinative dynamic action. This is James' tough-mindedness expressed in the personal religious concern of immanency. Man is related to the ultimately significant; God does give himself.

Within their peculiar cultural situation, however, the Greeks associated this affirmation of life with tragedy and destruction. Dionysus asserted the ultimate significance of process, and process includes the alternation of destruction and renewal. This particular destructive association stands in contrast to the life affirming symbol in the agriculturally oriented Canaanite society. Yet both stand for the same basic need for man's participation in meaningfulness. Both symbolize the declaration that the ultimately significant is process open to the future. Both suggest that it does make a difference that an individual person has lived, for he really does have options and really can change things. Dionysus stands for the fact that life is affirmed by being lived. Man is related to the ultimately significant, to God, and he can help to determine what is to be.

The belief that man has some of the divine within him is a religious expression of the belief that he can actualize the world. This is the symbolical uniting of man with the powers of creation and destruction. Against the structural principle of Apollo, the Orphic invention of the mysteries of Dionysus, for instance, seems to assert that man has a twofold nature, part divine and part human.[83] Man can be like the gods. The Titans, the gods of Tartarus and the old enemies of Zeus, gave toys to the infant god Dionysus, and while his attention was thus distracted, they set upon him and killed him. They then feasted on his flesh. In anger Zeus hurled a thunderbolt to burn them up and from the soot of the Titans and the divine Dionysus arose the race of man.[84] Thus Olympiodorus exhorts: we "must not take our own lives, since our bodies have in them something of Dionysus: for we are particles of him, since at the least we consist of Titanic soot and the Titans feasted on his flesh." [85]

The history of Dionysus, his origin and his development, is a vexing problem, but fortunately I have no need to make a pretense at solving it. All that I need to affirm is with Pentheus, that:

Scarce had I crossed our borders, when mine ear
Was caught by this strange rumour, that our own
Wives, our own sisters, from their hearths are flown
To wild and secret rites; and cluster there
High on the shadowy hills, with dance and prayer
To adore this new-made God, this Dionysus,
Whate'er he be! [86]

That is, I only need to affirm that Dionysus is a part of Greek life and that he has some of the immanent characteristics that represent an expression of the need to participate in life.

However, because I am asserting that Dionysus, as well as Apollo, represents an expression of a need found in essential man, it is relevant to the argument of this book to look for an earlier witness than Euripides. Otherwise, it seems, it would be difficult to talk about this need as an expression of a type of personality that is forever part of man's nature. The logical source is Homer; however, Rohde says "the Homeric poems hardly give any hint of that

23

overflowing of religious emotions which later Greek people knew and honored as a heaven-sent madness." He later directly associates this madness with Dionysus: It "had its origin in the religion of Dionysus and in company with this religion enters as something new and strange into Greek life." [87] In other words, he is saying that there is "hardly any hint" of Dionysus and for what he stands in Homer. In the light of what Homer himself has to say, this use of the phrase "hardly any hint" might be a little too extreme. In the *Iliad* when Zeus is recounting his love affairs, and their by-products, he refers to "Semele [who] bore Dionysus to give pleasure to mankind." [88] Earlier in the same tale he is even more informative. The mortal Lycurgus has had a quarrel with the gods of heaven and has "chased the Nurses of the frenzied Dionysus through the holy hills of Nysa, and the sacred implements dropped to the ground from the hands of one and all." Dionysus then "fled and found sanctuary under the salt sea waves." As a result "the immortals, easy livers as they are, resented what he had done" and Zeus struck Lycurgus blind.[89] In sum, then, Homer reveals that Dionysus is, in some regards at least, one of the immortals (for why else would the Olympians be resentful of Lycurgus and why else would Zeus take action), that he gives pleasure to mankind, that he has nurses, that he is frenzied, and finally, that he is present with his nurses in some way during their sacred rites.[90]

It seems to be true, then, that Dionysus was an element on the Greek scene, at least by the time of Homer, and with somewhat the same immanent characteristics that so marked him later on: creator of frenzy and giver of pleasure to mankind. In fact the evidence might even read that this immanent form of worship, which may or may not have included Dionysus by name, is among the oldest possessions of Greek religious faith and is chronologically older than the Olympian transcendent religion of Homer. Cornford says that "The religion of Dionysus is believed to have come into Greece from Thrace and Macedonia at least as early as the tenth century B.C. It was a form of worship more primitive and popular than the Olympian theology of Homer." [91]

This more primitive and popular Dionysus, who was not many hundred years younger than the Baal of the Ugaritic texts, was perhaps, like Baal, fundamentally a fertility deity. Although a late source, Euripides explicitly relates Dionysus to Demeter:

> Two spirits there be,
> Young Prince, that in man's world are first of worth.
> Demeter one is named; she is the Earth—
> Call her which name thou wilt!—who feeds man's frame
> With sustenance of things dry. And that which came
> Her work to perfect, second, is the Power
> From Semele born. He found the liquid shower
> Hid in the grape.[92]

Plutarch says the Greeks considered him as their "lord of the humid nature." [93] In the *Hymn to Dionysus* he is addressed as "ivy-tressed uproarious Dionysus." [94] Elsewhere in the *Bacchae* Dionysus himself says: "I have set my green and clustered vines to robe it round." [95] Later he gives man the "grief assuaging vine," that Euripides explicitly relates to the grape.[96] About his person the people wove rituals and created myths. For instance, some scholars believe that the re-enactment of his wanderings, deeds, and sufferings, as expressed in Euripides' *Bacchae*, had magical connotations that ensured the fertility of the land for the coming year.[97] Of course, this is not unique. The ceremonies performed in honor of Baal may have had the same effect, as were those performed in honor of Demeter, the goddess "that bears the seasons, the giver of goodly crops." [98] The important thing, however, is not whether Dionysus actually was a fertility deity, but that he has some related characteristics and so expresses the fundamental need of man to believe that he really plays a role in re-creation, that his actions and desires and enthusiasms really have an ultimate effect on reality. In religious terms, man believes that when in "sympathy" with nature he can affect or control the powers of nature. The *a priori* assumption is that there is a connection, a relationship between the supernatural and the natural, between the immortal and the mortal, and that action in one place has an effect on the other.[99]

Whatever their origin, there is a primitive expression of something in Greece similar to that directed toward Baal; and Greek tradition associated this non-rational, immanental need, which assumes the relative involvement of the divine that ritual and later drama expresses, with Dionysus. That this need was there and was expressed is evident. In the *Bacchae* one of the raving maenads says: "The simple nameless herd of humanity hath deeds and faith that are truth enough for me." Aristophanes implies that the Greeks universally knew about the cult of Dionysus.[100] Guthrie quite emphatically says that it was a "race of aristocrats who saw in the Olympians their fit and proper objects of worship," but it was Dionysus and related fertility gods who "remained as they have always done, close to the heart of the people." [101]

In the final Greek understanding of Dionysus it is interesting to note that just as Apollo, the symbol representing structure and order, revealed a receptivity toward participation and concern with life by taking over Delphi, and thereby became a transcendent deity using immanent means to advance his particular concern, so Dionysus, the symbol representing participation and process, revealed a receptivity toward distance, and the detached but ordered forms. He did this by accepting the performance of Greek drama as a valid expression of worship. The dramatists especially

26

created the choral dithyramb for the purpose of doing him honor. This was a sort of "passion play" expressing the passionate sufferings undergone; but by its very production as a "play" it found room for the detached observation and contemplation of the observer. Dionysus, the god of tragic participation, becomes the god of the form of Greek tragedy, just as Apollo, the god of the form of law and order, becomes the god participating in the administration of law and order. Apollo takes up and uses Delphi; Dionysus takes up and uses the drama.

The majesty of these Greek attempts to find a place for both needs, for man's full nature, anticipates our next observations on co-acceptance. However, we can say now that co-acceptance does not mean the compromising of the individual need which is responsible for the personality of the individual god. Dionysus still expresses, as Rohde says, something of "the common nature of mankind." [102] It is the need man has to feel that he belongs to the world and that his cares, desires, decisions and actions really have significance. The world is a different place because of this or that action. Man must feel that he plays a role in the world's tomorrow; that he helps create it. Its foundation is the acceptance of flux and process as ultimately significant, as being the primal thing that really is. Apollo, too, continues to express something else in the common nature of mankind. This is the need man has, to feel that there is something meaningful, something ultimately standing, that is beyond the "slings and arrows of outrageous fortune." Man must feel that there is some transcendent purpose or structure to the world that in some way is beyond our whims and desires, that in some way is valid, whether we are fortunate enough to see it or not. It is this ultimately valid structure that lends validity to our objectives in this world. It is the certain in an uncertain world, the Good, True and Beautiful that stand as a guide and goal for our striving natures.

It was not enough for the Greeks to see their gods being practically receptive to each other. They had to express the co-acceptance in their myths, as did the Canaanites. In both traditions a great deal is made of the struggle between the gods. But note that in neither tradition has the symbolical mythical representation ended in the struggle continuing on, or in the submission of one deity to the other. Despite a complete presentation of El's resistance to Baal, the Canaanite myth has El finally pouring dust on his head and mourning the death of Baal. This is the religious expression of a reconciliation of these two divergent attitudes of mind. So Greek myths describe a reconciliation. It was Apollo, at Delphi, who entered into the closest alliance with the Hellenized Dionysus and dared to introduce him into localities where he had hitherto been a stranger.[103] He even shared the shrine with him. Plutarch says "Bacchus also . . . has no less to do with Delphi than Apollo himself." [104] In the winter months the people believed that Apollo left Delphi to spend his time among the Hyperboreans, thereby allowing them "for three months to invoke Bacchus instead of Apollo." [105] During that time "to Dionysus or Bacchus they sing dithyrambic verses, full of passions and change, joined with a certain wandering and agitation backwards and forwards." This form of song was in sharp contrast to that song sung the other nine months of the year for "to Apollo they sing the well ordered paeon and a discrete song." [106] Thus again, even at the same shrine the contrast between the two gods stands out. To Dionysus the people sing a song of passion, change, agitation, and wandering. To Apollo they sing a song of order and discreteness. One song possesses, the other only addresses.

Greece has found room for the immanent as did Canaan. Apollo, the spokesman of Zeus, has accepted Dionysus. El has accepted Baal. Pausanias now can look at the images on the altar and see "wrought in relief . . . Zeus and Hermes . . . conversing; near stand Dionysus and Semele with Ino by her side." [107] He can look also at the Parthenon and see Dionysus among the seated gods. The Greeks accepted Dionysus, but he is still the god of one type of personality as Apollo is still the god of the other type. Plutarch cites other evidence besides dithyrambic and paeon verse. "Apollo both in their sculptures and statues they [the Greeks] always make to be young and never declining to old age; but Dionysus they represent in many shapes and forms." In a word, "to the one they attribute equality, order, and unmixed gravity; but to the other, a certain unequal mixture of sports, petulancy, gravity, and madness." [108]

CHRISTIANITY

The wisdom of the religious message might well be this co-acceptance. El accepts Baal, Apollo accepts Dionysus, yet El and Baal, Apollo and Dionysus still stand for basic divergent needs that man must express. Within its monotheism, I might perhaps give one more rather daring example of this co-acceptance of divergent needs as legitimate expressions of the ultimate explanation of things from the personal religious point of view. It is Christianity.[109] We certainly should expect a similarity if the argument of this book is valid, but we should also expect that the peculiar cultural concern of Christianity should introduce significant differences. This means that we cannot simply equate the immanent need as expressed in Christianity with Baal and Dionysus, or with the philosophical term process. Nor can we simply equate the transcendent need as expressed in Christianity with El and Apollo or with the philosophical term structure. But the argument of this book does assert that Christianity, and the worship of Baal and of Dionysus, and the idea of process, all symbolize an immanent need that is a common aspect of humanity, just as the transcendent expression which

29

we find in Christianity, the worship of El and Apollo, and the idea of structure, symbolize another common aspect of humanity.

The Christian attempt to express these two needs in an ultimate way is by its theological definition of the Godhead as Father and Son. The unique cultural emphasis of Christianity on sin and redemption determines the particular character and function of the expressions. Sinful humanity represents the fallen state which man must observe and contemplate, while redemption and eternal salvation represent the possibilities of a new and changed meaningful process. The Father represents the need for a transcendent judge acknowledging the sinful status quo, while the Son represents the need for an immanent lover acknowledging meaningful life and hope.[110]

The technical definition of "one ousia, three hypostases" is the Eastern Church's explanation of how to reconcile these two divergent expressions in the one God.[111] *Ousia* is the basis of the definition. The distinction between it and *hypostasis* is the same as that between the common and the particular. The one *ousia* preserves the single definition of existence while the *hypostases* assert the three particular expressions of existence.

> The Godhead is common; the fatherhood particular. We must therefore combine the two and say: "I believe in God the Father." The like course must be pursued in the confession of the law so we must combine the particular with the common and say, "I believe in God the Son." . . . Hence it results that there is a satisfactory preservation of the unity by the confession of the one Godhead, while in the distinction of the individual properties regarded in each there is the confession of the particular properties of the persons.[112]

30

In other words this view lodges the incomplete character-istics of immanency and transcendency with the particular *hypostasis,* Son and Father, and the totality of the two types of mental make-up in the one *ousia,* the Godhead. The Eastern Church's peculiar emphasis is always on the particular *hypostasis,* on God the Father and God the Son. Though this has the inherent danger of compromising Chris-tianity's monotheism, it does effectively preserve the real expression of each type of personality, and in the last analy-sis, the complete awareness of the need to find these expres-sions united in the ultimately significant.[113] Thus Eastern Christianity expresses in symbolical representation the par-ticular need to feel that life is meaningful and that an indi-vidual really plays an effective role in the formation of the world as well as the particular need to feel that there is a certainty and a meaning that judges these efforts to so form the world.

In the Christian West the church attempted the recon-ciliation of the two approaches and their resultant concepts by the technical definition "one substance, three persons." Substance is the basis of this definition as *ousia* was of the other. Here the church equated substance with essence and so the more technically correct Western expression is three persons of the same essence.[114] Superficially it is saying the same thing as does the East, but it fails to answer as effec-tively the demands of the two divergent types of personality. This is because of the shift of emphasis from the real exist-ence of the symbols for the divergent types of mental make-up which borders on tritheism, to an emphasis on the real existence of the theologically revealed One. The formulation now has no place within its confines for the ultimately sig-nificant Son as distinct from the ultimately significant Father. As a result it dangerously undermines the Christian attempt to give full expression to the two divergent but fundamental needs. This is clearly revealed when Augustine attempts to explain why the Father is the father, the Son is the son, and why they are different from each other: "The word of God, then, the only begotten Son of the Father, in all things like and equal to the Father, God of God, Light of Light, Wisdom of Wisdom, Essence of Essence, is altogether that which the Father is, yet is not the Father because the one is Son, the other is Father." [115] Quite simply this is saying that the Father and the Son are different just because one is one and is not the other.

The end result of the Christian attempt to absorb into one Godhead the need man has to believe that the universe is open to his reconstructive activities, and the need he has to believe that the universe itself yet restricts and directs those reconstructive activities, has met with philosophical success in the East, and has met with, at the most, a questionable philosophical success in the West. Perhaps this is why the congregations of the more traditional Western churches have lost the feeling of relatedness to the Godhead. Because of their inability to find an explanation as to why the Son is the Son, he tends to lose his identity within the Godhead, and that for which he stands, the need to feel one's role in life is really constructive and that there is a relation between God and man, becomes lost. In other words, for people tied to the Augustinian explanation of the Trinity, the Son is becoming more and more other-worldly, more and more the eternal lawgiver and less and less the lover. As a result, this explanation has forced some of them to evoke the immanent need anew. The cry now is to one who out of her motherly love truly understands man's plight and who, because of the intimate relation between a mother and her son, has a high degree of intercessory power. "Holy Mary, mother of God, pray for us sinners now and at the hour of our death, Amen." This tendency to substitute Mary for the Son who is becoming too "godlike" is an example of the expression of the need man has to feel that he is in touch with the powers of the universe and can change his fate. If his traditional concepts of the divine no longer reach him in his existential situation and no longer speak to him from his inherent needs, then he will create new ones.

Whether Christianity succeeds or not, its doctrine of the Trinity is an attempt to find room within its concept of what is ultimately significant in the world for expression of both types of needs. It is equivalent to asserting that any explanation of the universe must consider that universe in totality. We have also seen this in the final teaching of the Greek and Canaanite religions. They all find room within their understanding for all of nature's needs. Their final message is co-acceptance, but understood as a co-acceptance in an ultimately plural form. These two expressions of divergent needs are never reduced to one. Polytheism quite directly expresses them in terms of a plural pantheon; monotheism, with its more difficult task, expresses them in terms of aspects or natures of God. Dionysus and Apollo, Baal and El, God the Son and God the Father, may sit together in a temple frieze, live together in a people's myth, or be invoked in the same prayer, but they can never be absorbed into a simple unity. They are, so to speak, nature's two sides. We shall now see whether philosophy, and especially James and Dewey, in painting its house, heeded nature's message as well as did religion. First we ask, does philosophy have both sides? Second, does philosophy, in so far as it tries to understand the universe, endlessly deny one side or the other, or does it too finally end in co-acceptance, a polarized acceptance?

CHAPTER II

PROCESS VERSUS STRUCTURE IN THE CRITIQUE OF THE METAPHYSICS OF WILLIAM JAMES AND JOHN DEWEY

In order to carry out the objective of showing a congruence between religion and philosophy it is now necessary to take a close look at philosophy. The immediate objective is to see if it too expresses the same needs as does religion but, of course, in its less personal terminology. Do the poles immanent and transcendent, as represented more or less in Baal and El, Dionysus and Apollo, God the Son and God the Father, reappear in the philosophical terms process and structure? The previous chapter pointed out that in most respects an immanent god seems to be open to man's activities whereas in most respects the transcendent god seems to be beyond man's influence. The former is an expression of man's need to feel that he participates in the process of things and that his life is ultimately significant. The latter is an expression of man's need to feel that there is some sort of a measure reaching beyond the process of things, keeping it within bounds, restricting just what can be and cannot be done with human vitality. The first expression accepts the encountered world as ultimately significant, as process, whereas the second expression accepts eternal, restrictive principles as ultimately significant, as structure.[1]

However, before beginning to develop the closer look at philosophy, a word of warning: This philosophical in-

34

vestigation will not center about various philosophies as the religious investigation centered about various religions. This is because religion and philosophy, in so far as they are expressions of human needs flowing from types of personalities, historically express themselves in a different manner. A religion embodies of its very nature a group expression whereas a philosophy represents a single expression. A school of philosophy represents a collection of like minds and so theoretically may be only one possible insight into the nature of what is of ultimate significance in the world. A religion generally represents a collection of dissimilar minds originally united in some previous and other than religious association. This means that the basis for a group of philosophers' associating intellectually is a common viewpoint toward the world, whereas the most frequent basis for a group of religious devotees associating in religion has been until modern times on a common national, social or even lingual basis. Theoretically, this means that dissimilar needs are expressed within a religion and not so within a philosophy. Religion expresses its cross-section of needs by its different types of gods within the over-arching national religion; philosophy expresses the cross-section of needs by its different schools of philosophy.

Taking this warning to heart means that the argument of this book in all probability could receive its hearing by the study of the schools of philosophy representing all philosophical expressions within a particular era. The important thing would be to make sure that the philosophical expressions of the needs stemming from both types of personality would be captured for analysis. There is, however, another way to ensure the capturing of the complete philosophical expression of the two needs within an age, and that is to investigate a prevalent and controversial philosophy of a period and to consider it in conjunction with the criticism leveled against it from all sources. If the particular philosophical school is truly central and controversial, it seems that this latter possibility for study will reveal a more complete picture of philosophical expression than the former. For this reason, and because criticism of somebody else's philosophy always brings out rather sharply what a philosopher expects from a philosophy, I chose this latter possibility. The particular controversial philosophy which this book will consider is pragmatic naturalism, a school of thought which determined most issues discussed in our American philosophical journals until very recently. The particular expressions of that school studied are William James' and John Dewey's. In summary then, the premise that stimulated this chapter is the following: As the Greek and Canaanite myths represent a heterogeneous group attempting to relate themselves within a national unity to what they consider to be ultimately significant in the universe, so the critical debate over pragmatic naturalism represents a heterogeneous group attempting to express what they consider to be ultimately significant in the universe.[2]

Both William James and John Dewey were primarily interested in method. James' methodological postulate and Dewey's empirical method insisted, in principle, on James' statement that "nothing shall be admitted as fact except what can be experienced at some definite time by some experient." [3] As they developed it, this meant that we must trace back the products of refined methods to their origin in primary experience and that we must bring back the conclusions of secondary methods to the things of ordinary experience. In other words, the method we use to obtain knowledge is related to the end product of knowledge. All discussion must hinge upon some practical or particular issue of experience. We must do some thing and then experience its results. The end product validates the process, as it represents satisfaction of that process.

Dewey worked out the method and its implications in much greater detail than did James; yet in the eyes of the critics, and in reality, his development did not deviate from the fundamental principles held by James. Dewey adheres to the implications of James' basic assertion that "there can be no difference anywhere that doesn't make a difference elsewhere—no difference in abstract truth that doesn't express itself in a difference in concrete fact and in conduct consequent upon that fact, imposed on somebody, somehow, somewhere, and somewhen." [4] He insists that thinking inherently involves action, at least to the extent that it attempts to solve the problem which instigates the thinking process. Also he insists that the process or method is generative and creative because the active organism partly constitutes what is known. Its end product is a genuine additive event, a verification of the process which created it. For Dewey thinking becomes inquiry and its ideas become the intellectual instruments of inquiry which find their validity in what they effect or accomplish. [5]

Therefore, James' and Dewey's philosophical attempt to understand the world in which they live starts from experience and insists upon receiving verification from experience. To this extent they conceived the ultimately significant in the world to be the experienced flowing world of everyday activity. The real is here and nowhere else. It is changing nature. To them it seems that philosophy must direct its attention to what is and what can be, and its formulas must have practical significance. Philosophy must be organized about a naturalism with pragmatic method.

By understanding the task of philosophy in these terms and using "facts" as the foundation of its constructions rather than "principles," James' and Dewey's philosophical attempt in matters of method became "tough-minded." Because they started with the tough-minded facts and the open possibility of things, because they recognized instinct, fancy, and aspiring desire as weapons to accomplish happiness in the world, the philosophical critics have seen their joint efforts as an assertion of the validity of self-expression and a challenging of the place for structure, which the critic considered to be of at least equal value. Therefore, the issue between the critic and pragmatic naturalism centers not merely upon how well the pragmatic naturalist understands the whole world, but more precisely on whether his particular assertion of the ultimate significance of becoming or process as part of that world does in fact undermine structure. All of the critics are concerned, in other words, with structure. Some of them are quite receptive to finding a place for process in their total system and some of course deny any significance to it whatsoever, but all unite in being quite fearful that pragmatic naturalism is a one-sided philosophy of change and that a defense of structure is necessary. Edward Gleason Spaulding is an example. He reveals his concern for structure when he considers the pragmatic naturalist emphasis on the relatedness of the process of knowledge to the object of knowledge. He claims that the issue whether you are a pragmatic naturalist or not is to be settled on this very point. The precise question the thinker must answer is "whether or not knowing qûa knowing modifies or constitutes its object." [6] The fact that he sees the issue in these terms suggests that he understands the object of knowledge as an object to be a part of the structure of reality, and that any modification of it undercuts that structure. He is fearful that the assertion of process here means denial of structure.

Under these circumstances it is hard to agree that concern with F. J. E. Woodbridge's question "do what things are and the ways they operate depend on the eventuation of inquiry?" [7] is "simply a question of what thinking is and does in the world and how it gets its character of truth and falsity, wherever it occurs." [8] It is more significant than this. The existence of the question suggests that any critic concerned with this point thought that the pragmatic naturalist's assertion that knowing modifies the object of knowledge meant that this philosophy concerned itself only with modification and change, and that it undercut structure by demanding a relationship between the process of thinking

38

and the things of this world. H. C. Brown points out the significance of this question when he asserts that this is the very point critics need to dwell upon, for on it pragmatic naturalism "stands or falls. If we once grant that sensations are not elements out of which perceptions are composed, constituted or constructed; but that they are the finest most carefully discriminated objects of perception the rest [referring to Dewey's logical construction in his *Essays in Experimental Logic*] follows inevitably as we read on in the language of facts." [9]

This, then, is the significant issue. Pragmatic naturalism affirms becoming, and Our Critics (no matter of what school) affirm structure. In sympathy some may say, along with Royce, that "we are . . . all of us, more or less pragmatists," but all will agree with his assertion that the really determining question is what place is that side of our doctrine going to occupy in the whole body of our convictions? [10] If the pragmatic side dominates, we have a doctrine concerned first and last with change and becoming, for it is the "voice of those whose philosophy is inspired by a discontent with things as they are and who believe that it is the special business of the mind to change them." [11] The danger seen in this side dominating is that it will transfer the seat of intellectual authority to the "arts of practical guidance and control." [12] Now nature will become entirely relative to human concern and there will be no room for external authority. According to George Santayana, pragmatic naturalism uses "its past as a stepping stone, or rather as a diving board, but has an absolutely fresh will at each moment to plunge this way or that into the unknown. The universe is an experiment, it is unfinished. It has no ultimate or total nature, because it has no end. It embodies no formula or statable law; any formula is at best a poor abstraction, describing what, in some region and for some time, may be the most striking characteristic of existence; the law is a description *a posteriori* of the habit things have chosen to acquire, and which they may possibly throw off together." [13] In essence, pragmatic naturalism has a vital momentum but no predetermined goal. It regards nature "as a landscape that paints itself." It is so afraid of getting somewhere it does not ask where it is going.[14] It represents an excessive romantic emphasis on freedom, vitality, life and going rather than on what to do with that freedom or where to go with that vitality. As a result, Morris Cohen says, it "reflects the temper of an acquisitive society feverishly intent on mere accumulation, and morally afraid to discriminate between what is worthwhile and what is not. The same preference for terms of promiscuous all-inclusiveness, rather than for those that involve the discrimination essential to philosophic clarity, shows itself also in the use of the terms experience and reality." [15]

A more specialized way of expressing the same overall point is Ralph Barton Perry's statement that the pragmatic naturalist "emphasizes the adventure of verification to the neglect of that in which verification consists." [16] Santayana caustically adds: it "is an external view only, which marks the place and conditions of the mind in nature, but neglects its specific essence: as if a jewel were defined as a round hole in a ring." [17] It is a product, says John Russell, of a twofold confusion which "confounds the situation in which thinking and knowing arise, with truth and knowledge themselves, . . . [and which] confounds the consequences, the practical experiences to which truth leads, with truth itself." [18] All of these comments about pragmatic naturalism, from Josiah Royce's concern with its due place to John Russell's declaration that it confuses experiences to which truth leads with truth itself, assume that pragmatic naturalism is only a partial outlook on life and, therefore, incomplete. These critics may assert that becoming or process has a place, but their insistence is that there must be structure over and above it. Quite simply the criticism is

40

that the pragmatic naturalistic concern is only with activity and method. It has no interest in ends and directions.

It is interesting to note that W. H. Sheldon has attempted to express the issue as Our Critics see it, in terms of "needs." He declares that the side we choose depends upon the answer we give to the question: "What need does philosophy attempt to meet?" Sheldon says the critic of pragmatic naturalism bases his philosophy of life on the contemplative need "of a knowledge of the character, on broadest lines,— of our universe," while the pragmatic naturalist bases his view of life on "the other great instinct, . . . that for practical welfare." By making the division in these terms Sheldon identifies the need for meaningful change and function with the need for making society more congenial to our practical interests. His own personal view is that both "needs" are natural and therefore ultimately significant. A true philosophy, therefore, must take in consideration both emphases.[19] Of course, his statement assumes that pragmatic naturalism only concerns itself with change and becoming and to this extent he is here in agreement with the critics. He also comes dangerously close to the implication that the pragmatic concern for practical welfare is a different matter from the critical concern for contemplation of the universe on its broadest lines. This would in effect deny the objective value of the pragmatic concern as he understands it. But perhaps more significant is his use of the term "needs." This is really a concession to what pragmatic naturalism asserts, for it assumes that not only do the needs of a human organism contribute to the understanding of the world but that they are a natural part of that universe as well.

John Herman Randall, Jr. takes somewhat the same position regarding this concept of need when he says that philosophy is a sort of watered down mythology, one "grown less colorful and more respectable." As with myth, man creates it for the purpose of satisfying his needs. It must enable him to "control and change his surroundings to make the actual world he lives in a better place in which to dwell and it must furnish him with an ideal world which can make his struggles worthwhile, which can console him for his failures, and spur him to new successes." It "must build a heaven into which man may escape if need be, and draw fresh inspiration; and it must furnish him with the architect's plans. . . . It must provide the incentive, and indeed the final goal of life; and it must provide the means to the achievement of some measure of heavenly beauty on the drab fields of earth." [20] As Randall sees it, the pragmatic view flows from the function or need of creating new facts in the world of existence, and the critics' view flows from the function or need of creating an ideal world congenial to man's own personality in order to make the pragmatic view worthwhile.

W. P. Montague carries this dualistic emphasis further and asserts that since pragmatic naturalism represents satisfaction of a need, and the critical view represents satisfaction of another need, it may well be that the two philosophical approaches do not conflict but represent two expressions of concern for two different types of problems. He is reiterating the critical emphasis that pragmatic naturalism is only partially complete as well as making the additional assertion that Sheldon and Randall resist making, namely, that pragmatic naturalism does not deal with the same fundamental matter as the critics' philosophy. The pragmatic naturalistic concern is "how we should get our knowledge and how we should test its truth." The critical concern is "the nature of the relation of a knower to the object known." [21] At first glance, this seems to be sound enough. In fact, William James asserted as much at times, but just as he and Dewey at the very least implied a philosophy of nature, so a further look at the two problems shows them to be interwoven to such an extent that the solution of one need and its problems naturally affects the other need and its problems.

For example: if we assert that we get our knowledge via the process of inquiry and that the test of truths that are its object rests on its relationship to the process, we are asserting that there is an essential relationship between the knower who affects the process of inquiry and the object known. The opposite also is true; if we assert that we get our knowledge via a process of inquiry but that the truths that are its object do not rest in the relationship to the process but in something apart from the process, we are asserting that the knower does not have an essential relationship to the object known.

A. W. Moore's more concrete example of good and bad wheels might help to make this point a more effective example of the impossibility of Montague's efforts to take these two needs and consider them as exclusive concerns which have no ultimate metaphysical connection.[22] If we distinguish the two types of wheels from each other on the basis of their relation to automobiles, or watches, or wagons, we are asserting Sheldon's and Randall's concern for practical welfare. The good wheel is that which does best what we want it to do. This functional description of good and bad is an expression of Montague's pragmatic naturalistic concern for "how we should get our knowledge and how we should test its truth," and it represents an attempt to satisfy that need. However, this answer also involves Montague's critical concern for "the nature of the relation of a knower to the objects known," because it asserts the essential relationship between the good wheel and the knower of the good wheel who associates it with its context and, therefore, makes it good. This interrelation of Montague's two concerns is also evident if we distinguish the good wheel from the bad wheel on the basis of "contemplation and adoration of the celestial essence of circularity." We are still involved with the pragmatic naturalist concern of how we should get our knowledge and how we should test its truth, for we are asserting the existence of an ideal world

43

which possesses the truth we must recognize. But just as the pragmatic concern which considered the wheels as good or bad depending upon their function involved the critical concern for the relation of knower to the objects known, so also the pragmatic concern in this instance involves the critical concern of "the nature of the relation of the knower to the object known." This is so because we are asserting necessarily that the ideal good or bad wheel stands completely apart from the knower who knows that ideal. In this case we must recognize rather than make the goodness or badness of the wheels. It stands apart from the functional needs of our automobile, or watch, or wagon, and the knower knowing it plays no part in its being good or bad.

The conclusion can only be that Montague fails when he asserts that pragmatic naturalism's concern for process and Our Critic's concern for structure can co-exist on different ontological levels. Therefore, if it is true that the critical view and the pragmatic naturalistic view do flow from different "needs," these "needs" must both be rooted in the nature of what is ultimately significant in the world.

NEED FOR AFFIRMATION OF STRUCTURE

In effect, what the above critics in their attack on pragmatic naturalism have done is first to label it as a partial philosophy receptive only to the needs of change and process, and then seriously to question whether this awareness is of real significance in trying to understand the universe. To them it seems pragmatic naturalism is a philosophy that generally wishes to interpret not only animate nature but the whole world on an anthropomorphic model; moreover, to some it seems a philosophy that tends to "reduce the human ego to a stream of consciousness in which personal identity is minimal." [23]

In order to balance this partial view, R. W. Sellars asserts that a true philosophy must be receptive to the need of structure and being, "the formal, the structural, the timeless." Of course, it is possible to stress too exclusively either of these needs but it seems "as in most controversies, a middle position is more likely to be right." [24] He does not assert, as did W. P. Montague, that the two needs are concerned with different separate problems, but that there are two needs and that we must consider both so that we can adequately recognize each. Morris Cohen emphatically supports this when he says that "universality and individuality, justice and the law, the ideal and the actual, are inseparable, yet never completely identifiable. Like being and becoming, unity and plurality, rest and motion, they are polar categories. Deny one and the other becomes meaningless. Yet the two must always remain opposed." [25] All of human effort is a tension between these polar categories or needs, "one to do justice to the fullness of the concrete case before us, the other to grasp an underlying abstract universal principle that controls much more than the one case before us." [26]

Cohen's own particular construction of a philosophy that does give ultimate space to each pole is interesting. He bases his philosophy on the awareness that in modern experimental and mathematical physics the tendency now is to find the element of permanence—"without which there would be no science"—in mathematical relations, rather than in the metaphysical notion of matter as an ultimate substance. He unites this understanding of structure with his doctrine of the two poles by asserting that "only a rationalistic naturalism can liberate us from false alternatives between means and ends. It does so by showing that logically the end or aim of any rational conduct is not something outside of our activity itself but a character or pattern of life itself." [27] His thesis is that change and constancy are strictly co-relative terms and that within the stream of life objects or individuals can maintain their character. This is true because the laws of logic and mathematics do hold for nature. It is with this assertion that Cohen lays bare his own particular attitude toward the two poles. It is one that allows little real significance for change and process. "The meaning of any notion does not itself move but is rather a timeless fact or phase of nature." [28]

Cohen's "rationalistic naturalism" becomes not an acceptance of the ultimate significance of the process we experience in nature so much as it becomes a rational attempt to decipher the timeless meanings in that nature. It is not an attempt to understand and accept nature; instead, it is an attempt to avoid the dictates of its crude changing character. "The difficulty in grasping . . . the significant aspect of nature is . . . simply the difficulty of leaving the ordinary practical interests in the personal possession or manipulation of things, and rising to a reflective insight as to what the world contains." Or even more powerfully stated, "It is the function of rational science as of art, religion, and all human effort to liberate us from the charnel house of the actual and reveal to us the underlying order which governs the wider realm of possibilities." [29]

F. J. E. Woodbridge also strikes out for a harmony between the two needs when he asserts that "structure and behavior may indicate ultimates in metaphysical analysis just as force and matter may." [30] He agrees with Cohen's rejection of matter as an ultimate substance when he says that matter as "a name for some hidden inherently changeless, everlasting permanent, and only apparently alterable material or substance or cause of the present world is a view I would avoid—not because I dislike it, but because I find it meaningless." [31] But he, as did Cohen, makes it evident that the balance between force and matter is truly one with a dominance given to structure. His "realms of being" are always the same, no matter where or when a philosopher is born and it is man's job in the cognitive business to discover laws to which the transformation of materials con

46

forms. Finally, although he asserts specific activity and specific structure go together, he also says "specific behavior is dependent on specific structure—meaning by dependence here that without the structure the behavior does not occur." [32]

Arthur O. Lovejoy might be a good example of a third critic who within his own context as philosopher attempts to construct a philosophy in harmony with both structure and process. Perhaps even more emphatically than Cohen and Woodbridge, he asserts the predominance of structure or plan of action, yet he too interprets that plan as "essentially a process, a sequence of complexes constantly developing one into another. And the process is . . . one of progressive organization having a selective or teleological character. The plan itself and the measures for its realization are gradually built up, through the bringing to either of such thought material as is recognized as having relevancy to the business at hand, and through the deliberate selection of some possible and nascent responses and the neglect or conscious repression of others." [33]

These critics who are receptive to the need for process and its place in understanding the world, and who think in terms of balance rather than in terms of either/or, are still proponents of a dominating structure when the pragmatic naturalistic claims confront them. They may think in terms of balance, but when so confronted they feel that in order to keep that balance they must become the champions of structure. Their cause becomes the demand for civilized control of enthusiasm. They agree with the less sympathetic critics who say that you cannot intelligently discuss the instruments of human progress unless you first know its goal. When carried to its logical conclusion, they agree that pragmatic naturalism finds itself involved in a *reductio ad absurdum,* for not everything can be instrumental; something must be final. The very nature of action demands stability. As W. E.

Hocking puts it: "All action intends to change something in particular: and in order to effect just the alteration in the world the frame of action must hold still! The maxim for action is: Regard the universe as static except where you want it to bridge. The ideal situation for the man who wants to move things is to have an unalterable conviction at his back: 'Here I stand, I can not otherwise, God help me.' The man who can say that will either make things happen or be himself obliterated." [34] The more sympathetic critic who believes that process is a valid aspect of the world is in agreement with the unsympathetic critic who will allow no place for process. Both believe that pragmatic naturalism has sacrificed structure, at least to some extent, and both champion the need for its revival. Only the more sympathetic critic may agree with Royce when he says "we must be pragmatists," but all will agree with his additional "but also more than pragmatists." This is what he means when he says that "although my predicates are, as pragmatism asserts, the constructions of the present moment, . . . the truth of my judgment is not a mere construction of the present moment, but belongs to the unity of the various constructive processes of momentary selves." [35]

Because of this attitude toward structure and because of the assumption that James and Dewey are only concerned with process and change, Our Critics, sympathetic and unsympathetic alike, when finding evidence of structure in James and Dewey, use this evidence to prove that even pragmatic naturalism in its partiality must contradict itself. W. H. Sheldon says that "the pragmatist can not help talking as if there were a reality where character does not in the least depend on our judgment." [36] B. H. Bode goes to great lengths to prove that "pragmatism tactily postulates an object of reference which lies beyond the experience of the individual." [37] Arthur O. Lovejoy says "that there are some truly coercive and indubitable truths, some items of *a priori* knowledge inhering in the native constitution of a

48

rational mind . . . [that even] James pretty fully and frankly declares." [38]

The battle lines are thus formed and there is no crossing over. As far as Our Critics see them, the pragmatic naturalists fail to answer Professor Randall's ideal need and so their mission is to assert its valid place in a total picture of philosophy. The call is always for structure in one form or other. Rationalism against naturalism, form against matter, stability against change, being against becoming, moderation against enthusiasm, sharp clear individuality against collective totality, classicism against romanticism.

I hope it is clear that I am not saying that all of the critics referred to in this chapter are classicists, or rationalists, or formalists. What I am saying is that as critics of pragmatic naturalism they are all espousing structure because they all believe, in one way or another, that the pragmatic naturalist has sacrificed it. As *critics* they are structuralists, or as James would say, "a priorists." They center their interest on recollection rather than on anticipation. They insist that life must have a background of authoritative categories upon which men may depend. These are to be the guides, pointers, or whatever you want to call them, that men use to direct themselves to better things. The critics' call is for men to turn their gaze upon these fixed categories rather than on temporal process. W. P. Montague claims that "the laws of space, number and of matter and energy have not changed from the times of Euclid and Pythagoras and Archimedes; the laws of gasoline engines were just the same in the days of the ancient Athenians as now. We know them and they did not." [39] Only these laws are worthy of our attention. If man would only look on them, says George Santayana, he could "recover the true although unrealizable ideals of the race." He would again "believe in harmony, in intelligence, in perfection and perhaps even in heaven." If he would look upon these unchanging principles he would at last reject "that romantic infatuation which for a century has been glorifying will, work, struggle, contradiction, and instability, without any idea or hope of an ultimate good." [40]

The single objective which drives the critics is even evident in a comment Dewey made about their criticisms: "I obtain a certain enjoyment from reading criticisms which combine condemnation of my 'pragmatism' for its alleged sacrifice of knowledge to practice with condemnation of my 'instrumentalism' for greatly exaggerating the potential function of knowledge and of intelligence in direction and enrichment of every day experiences." [41] Both of these particular criticisms stem from the general criticism that pragmatic naturalism has sacrificed the structural aspect of nature. Morris Cohen might be an example of a critic making the first form of criticism when he asserts that the pragmatic naturalist must admit the "obvious fact that the successful progress of any scientific investigation depends largely upon the initial or anticipatory ideas according to which it is instituted and according to which it proceeds." [42] Once we abolish this fixed starting point or goal definite direction and the constancy which we call the identity of the object goes, and then nothing is left save the fact of motion. It is, therefore, necessary to assert that there is an exact determination of what is relevant in practical life and to assert that it is an affair of reason. Practical life must "submit to reason. Neither brute authority nor the immediacy of experience, neither mystic intuition nor unreasoned imagery form a sufficient basis for an adequate human philosophy. Always we need a rational apprehension of the significance of things in the relational or intelligible contexts." [43] The second criticism is closely related to the first, and certainly the same critic can make it and the first in the same paragraph. However, in order to exemplify this criticism, let us consider W. P. Montague's statement that "the only conceivable basis for an idea or a belief being generally and permanently useful is that it is true—true in the

50

realistic sense of conforming to or pointing to a reality that is in no sense created by it. If ideas or beliefs created their objects, the process of thought would be arbitrary; one belief would be as useful or rather as useless as another." [44] Perhaps E. B. McGilvary implies the same argument when he says "discovery is not invention." [45]

Thus, in simple terms the two criticisms come down to a demand that there be something more than the practical itself. Our Critics would prevent the sacrifice of knowledge to practice by being sure that initial or anticipatory ideas are always directing the practice. They would prevent the exaggeration of the role of knowledge in directing and enriching everyday experience by reminding the knower again and again that the function of knowledge is only to recognize what is true. In no sense does the knower create truth; he only recognizes it. Therefore, both criticisms assert that there is more than process in nature and this more is prior to the imperfect changing process in the sense that it "keeps thought from becoming blocked in its progress and holds it to an identifiable track." [46] Cohen asserts that there are anticipatory ideas independent of the process. Montague asserts that there are truths independent of the process. Both critics agree in their own way with Woodbridge's statement that "nature is teleological in fact. Her time scheme declares it, and our knowledge is dependent on it." [47] Nature has a plan, a force, a logic, a purpose, which we must take into account at both ends. In other words, both criticisms assert the place for Sheldon's and Randall's ideal need. Whether you call it this, or structure, or the moral order, or the sensible order, it is the call for form and moderation to control and to coerce the enthusiasm and becoming of the pragmatic naturalists. In the words of John Grier Hibben, "we may will to accomplish certain ends, but are under compulsion to use only certain means if we would be successful. The relation between the means and the definite end in question lies deep in the nature

51

of things, and is wholly independent of our will or wish. Our business is not to change this fundamental relation, and make it what we might like to have it, but to discover exactly what it is and to deal with it accordingly. We may regard ourselves as artists in the composition of the truth, but hardly as creators." [48]

In reiteration, the critics, regardless of what their relationship is to each other, attack the pragmatic naturalists because they are not satisfied with the latters' attempts to explain the structure of the universe. Whether it is valid or not, this common dissatisfaction has had the effect in debate of placing the pragmatic naturalists in the romantic camp and of placing the critics in the classical camp. It seems the pragmatists, who respond to the need to believe that process is significant, are determined to reconstruct the world, while the critics, who respond to the need to believe that there is a transcendent limitation to that process, search for ideals, checks and guides. Individually, although in varying degrees, the critics may agree that there is a "necessity of a revision of the conception of the fixed," and that "the fixed itself must be conceived dynamically." Collectively, as Our Critics, they look on pragmatic naturalism, along with Santayana, as "a radical romanticism which from the beginning of the world has been the philosophy of those who as yet had had little experience; for to the blinking child it is not merely something in the world that is new daily, but everything is new all day." [49]

CRITICISM OF JAMES' AND DEWEY'S CONCEPT OF CONTINUITY

James' and Dewey's refusal to give an existence to ideas prior to the process in which they are involved is perhaps the aspect of pragmatic naturalism that sums up most completely the character of that philosophy which the critics felt it was necessary to attack. As F. J. E. Woodbridge so clearly remarks: "Pragmatism, as I understand it, claimed or certainly seemed to claim, that apart from operation in discourse and experiment, ideas not only have no meaning, but are non-existent; and that, consequently, the function of ideas is not to represent, stand for, or duplicate objects in some way, but to mediate the processes of discourse and experiment. If I am not mistaken, it was this dogma which was the prime motivator of the controversy which ensued." [50] In Dewey's phrase, the issue is over the "fallacy of dogmatism," the habit of hypostatizing the conclusions to which reflection may lead, and depicting them as prior realities. For him, these conclusions are in reality nothing but meanings surrounding the passing experience. They are instrumental aids in leading action, and it is idolatrous to regard them as deep and powerful realities that produce the obvious objects of our everyday world and afterwards somehow reveal themselves, just as they are, to the thoughts of metaphysicians. They are only projects of solution, promissory and hypothetical in character. Their validity or truth consists in doing what they claim to do, namely, resolve difficulties, and in this sense they become verified.

Our Critics direct criticism at this point because they believe that rejection of the *a priori* ideas deals "a rude blow . . . at dogma of every sort: god, matter, Platonic ideas, active spirits, and creative logic all seem to totter on their thrones." [51] Thus, Santayana, a "realist," and Hocking, an "idealist," agree. When we remove the *a priori* as the producer of the reality we know and as that which verifies this reality, "there is no strictly immediate truth . . . there is no strictly stable or eternal truth . . . there is no a priori truth; and in sum . . . there can be no significant theoretical certainty." [52]

It is interesting to note that Santayana's further criticism clearly reveals his denial of ultimate significance to process. He claims that the decision between pragmtic naturalism and its critics is over method and metaphysics. On this point he might agree with Montague's attempt to present pragmatic naturalism as a philosophy concerned only with "how we should get our knowledge and how we should test its truth." The assumption is twofold: that process has no objectivity in the truly significant part of nature and that rejection of *a priori* disembodied powers and immaterial functions is automatically a rejection of all that we call metaphysical.[53] The fact that Santayana and Hocking make a similar criticism is perhaps more significant. (Here philosophers with little in common are united in the assertion that pragmatism sacrifices structure and that in order to defend this structure it is necessary to understand it as an *a priori* construction standing over and above nature's flow.) This is equivalent to the assertion of a dualism of process and that which controls it. The latter is an independent structure which itself is unchanging but which directs the change. The rational aspect of man, that aspect which transcends the flux of nature or, as Reinhold Niebuhr puts it, that aspect of man that is conscious of the fact that he is involved in the flux, and therefore is not in flux, discovers it.[54] Empirical method can find it when it is compelled "to use certain standard categories, e.g., permanent reality, causation. . . ." Yes, even the pragmatic naturalist with his *a priori* category of purpose asserts the need for control, but his refusal or failure to study these categories makes his thought "narrow and unphilosophical." [55] Sheldon continues the argument and says that it is these neglected categories that exert the control over the process and cannot themselves be altered in the process, otherwise nature is "dependent upon our momentary whim." [56]

Thus Our Critics insist that the demand for control necessitates the rational recognition of structure which is that part of reality which wields control. As we understand structure more and more, we progressively discover control; and, Professor Woodbridge observes, such "increased control reveals the ends, purposes, and use of nature as nothing else does. To be sure, it does not make clear to us, as some moralists seem to think it should, what we ought to do, but it does make strikingly clear to us what we might and also what it is utterly useless to try to do." [57] As the critic sees it, it is this desire to recognize control that marks him apart from pragmatic naturalism and puts him in step with scientific activity, defined by Morris Cohen as "the pursuit of the ideal of certainty, exactness, universality and system." [58]

In a general way this broad demand for an unalterable control over the altering process is the basis for all of the criticisms leveled against James and Dewey. In a specific way, however, we can consider it as a dualistic criticism of nature's continuity. This becomes clear when we look at Cohen's criticism of pragmatic naturalism. His thought takes full cognizance of the two needs, or poles as he calls them, in nature. Therefore, his irritation with pragmatism stems not from the fact of its recognizing the need of one pole or the other, but from its "gratuitously identifying two different poles of reality, viz., the absolute totality and immediate feeling, without providing the proper locus for the mediating relations." [59] He claims pragmatic naturalists are guilty of this, first, because they identify the universe with what we experience, thereby denying any reality to the objects of logical or conceptual thought; second, because they are so completely absorbed in human experience that it is impossible for them to formulate any adequate theory of non-human or physical nature.

Of course, Cohen goes on, concern with this pole is valid, for the principle of polarity indicates that nature is more than reason, that the actual world cannot contain form unless it contains irrational matter that has form. This is evident, for example, even in scientific method's "ultimate appeal to the observation of brute fact which natural science must employ in verification." [60] But the principle of polarity also indicates that we must not allow this physi-

55

cal need to change things, to swallow up the ideal, mental need. The two needs are interrelated but "we must, by all means, keep the distinction between the mental and the physical." [61] There is a dualism between these poles, not the "common dualism which conceives the mind and the external world as confronting each other like two mutually exclusive bodies" but the dualism of Aristotelian matter and form.[62] Recognition of this dualism, yet union, of possibility and actuality, of significance and fact, "enables us to see the rational or scientific role of the imagination, and saves us both from nearsighted positivism and the romantic capriciousness that wilfully blinds itself to the order of fact." [63] The argument is that once we accept the fact that these two poles do in fact exist and that they do demand gratification, it is the job of the intellect to effect a harmony between them. The pole labeled matter attempts to do justice to the fulness of the concrete case in nature, while the pole labeled form attempts to do justice to the underlying abstract universal principle that controls the individual concrete cases covered by the other pole.

A break in the pragmatic naturalistic continuity is evident here, and even more so when we further consider the formal pole in its related guise of "possibility" and "significance" as compared to the material understood as actuality and fact. The formal pole thus has *a priori* authority. Its propositions are the same for all regardless of the individual differences in the class to which they apply. Its rules of logic or pure mathematics universally apply to all propositions irrespective of differences of their material content. These rules of mathematics and logic ("the two . . . are identical in essence") [64] are of such authority because they are the prior laws according to which all objects or realities are combined. They exist independently of these objects or realities and are prior to them, although they need the latter to explore their possibilities.[65] This accounts for the formal pole's "possible" or "potential" label. It determines how realities can become. The additional label of "significance" means that not only does the process or matter receive its direction from the form, but it receives its verification from it. No natural proposition can pretend to scientific truth unless it submits to the formal relations. This is true on the personal level as well as on the level of intellectual discipline. All efforts must finally seek the invariant property amidst the flux. If we define philosophy as the attempt to deal with this invariant, with "the more general or constant phases of truth about nature," [66] then all effort must end in asking the philosophical question "why." Physics, the concern for the specific and the concrete, for example, must seek for an explanation of "why things are constituted or behave in their particular way" and empirical facts cannot satisfy it.[67]

The dualism that results is of natural phenomena and logically necessary relations, the latter standing independently of the former. This fact of independence destroys continuity and asserts the emphatic need for the unvarying structural pole controlling the dynamic changing pole.[68]

CRITICISM OF JAMES' AND DEWEY'S RECONSTRUCTED OBJECT OF KNOWLEDGE

The effort to assert that there must be more than nature's process or continuity culminated in the critics asserting the existence of a dualism of underlying abstract universal principles and individual concrete experiences. The critical assertion that in the process of knowing there must be certain fundamental principles whose existence is a presupposition of all knowledge has the same effect. But this time the dualism is even less sympathetic to the basic dynamic categories of pragmatic naturalism. Here again the issue is Dewey's "fallacy of dogmatism" and here again the effort is to elevate structure.

B. H. Bode says that the fundamental principles that we presuppose in the process of knowing are not simply devices by which we secure inner harmony, but "must necessarily be ultimate and underivable facts of our mental structure." [69] They are the fixed and independent matter which directs inquiry to solve its particular problems as well as being that which we finally know. They exist apart from the process of inquiry and that process neither constitutes nor essentially modifies them. To assert otherwise, says A. K. Rogers, is confusing the pychological analysis of the nature of experience with the original meaning of the knowing experience. Such confusion is fatal because it is saying that knowledge is no more than immediate transitional feelings and that all reality is no more than the immediate facts of psychological experiencing. This in effect is "the denial of that which underlies all knowledge alike as its original presupposition, and as a result we have brought the whole edifice of knowledge crashing down about our heads." [70] Our Critics feel the necessity for preventing the edifice from crashing down about our heads, and so of course they assert the existence of these pre-existing principles which underlie the concrete experiences of knowledge. The pragmatic naturalists may claim this makes their critics guilty of the "fallacy of dogmatism," but they are basing such a claim on a misinterpretation of that fallacy. "The great error of dogmatists in hypostatizing their conclusions into alleged preexistent facts," says Santayana,

> did not lie in believing that facts of some kind preexisted; the error lay only in framing an inadequate view of these facts and regarding it as adequate. God and matter are not any or all the definitions which philosophers may give of them: they are the realities confronted in action, the mysterious but momentous background, which philosophers and other men mean to describe by their definitions or myths or sensible images. To hypostatize these human symbols and identify them with matter or with God is idolatry:

but the remedy for idolatry is not iconoclasm, because the senses, too, or the heart of the pragmatic intellect, can breed only symbols. The remedy is rather to employ the symbols pragmatically with detachment and humor, trusting in the steady dispensations of the substance beyond.[71]

Aside from making the point that it is perfectly legitimate to believe in *a priori* mental constructions, there is the implication that the holder of the opposite view asserts only the existence of a foreground and that to him "knowledge is no more than immediate transitional feeling." Of course, Santayana and others have asserted this implication before. Its basis lies in the critics' assumption that the object of knowledge is part of nature's structure as known. Since the pragmatic naturalist claims that in a state of knowledge the knower knowing the object changes it, the critics therefore held he denied that nature has a structure. This again brings us to Spaulding's epistemological question of "whether or not knowing qûa knowing modifies or constitutes its object." In Santayana's words, are "the realities confronted in action" modified or simply described by that action? Fundamentally, the critic who declares that "knowing qûa knowing in no case modifies or constitutes its object" is trying to preserve an *a priori* real foundation for flux.[72] By implication, at least, he understands pragmatic naturalism as a philosophy in which a "half hearted and short winded" concept of nature dominates to the extent that it sees only a foreground, subservient to personal immediate feelings and to the extent that it answers special rational and cultural interests. He can assert protestingly that this "romanticism" is inverting nature by putting the accidental order of discovered foreground over and above nature's "natural order of genesis," above nature's dramatic unities of substance and essence.[73] His mission to defend the structural is as clear as that of the other critics. His particular concern is to assert the separation of the functional and the structural, the object known and the process by which the object became known and to assert that the structural controls that functional process, in effect to deny the possibility of true novelty.

Two philosophers who were rather vocal in their protests that there is no internal connection between the object known and the process by which we know the object are Edward Gleason Spaulding and Arthur O. Lovejoy. Although they differed between themselves they were united in opposing this concept of continuity. In this sense both were dualists. Spaulding attempts to prove that Dewey assumes, in at least one instance, that we can obtain genuine knowledge without its being in a context of process, without its genetic account. If we can prove this, he asserts, it is evident that some "things" do not have a genesis, that "there are certain logical facts . . . which not only are logically prior to any genesis, but are presupposed in any genuine knowledge of real genesis." [74] The example Spaulding uses to prove his point is the logic of proof, of classes or relations, and so forth. These principles are logically antecedent to the solving of questions of genesis. We presuppose them in all attempts to solve problems of genesis. "Logic is prior to both the genesis and the genetic account. For both the solution of the question and the occurence of the genesis which that solution describes, and the final attainment of a true result, presuppose certain logical principles which subsist prior to and independently of their being known and used. The fact that these questions of genesis may be studied antecedently in time to the study of logic does not make them logically antecedent." [75]

The effect of such a proof is, first, the denial of the intrinsic connection between process of inquiry and object of knowledge; second, the assertion of objects of knowledge that are unalterable, simple gems of reality having only an external relationship to being known, that is, which are "not modified, altered, or constituted by the knowing," and, third, the implication that these structural ideals are presupposed in such a way that they determine genetic accounts.[76]

A more definite presentation of essentially the same call for an unmodified structure to stand out against the flow of the physical realm is Professor Lovejoy's. Knowing is "a kind of foreign commerce, a trafficking with lands in which the traffickers do not live, but from which they may continually bring home good store of merchandise to enrich the here and now." [77] Dualism is so clear and obvious to Lovejoy that he even advances Dewey's "creative intelligence" in support. It is "quite as 'supernatural' as the dualistic epistemologist's 'representative ideas.' It may, in fact, be said to be more 'supernatural,' " for mere "representation" is a function which, though external to the system with which the natural sciences deal does not disturb the system, or limit the range of applicability of the law of those sciences. "But the control of 'things' by a unique, non-mechanistic process of 'intelligence'—nay, the creation of a new content of reality, the introduction into the physical order of genuine novelties, by man's reflection and contrivance—this is not a mere external addition to, but an interjection of a foreign element into the system of nature known to physical science." [78]

Lovejoy continues that an intelligent act is an act that makes contact with two lands, the here and now where we live and the other in which we do not live but which provides the good store of merchandise to enrich us. There must be both lands, one needing enrichment, one having the enrichment to give to the other. Otherwise there would be nothing to do and therefore no action. Action would not occur if that which we wanted to be done had already been done. "A plan of action would not be a plan of action if that which it contemplates existed, or were already going on, in the physical world; for a plan requires to be realized."

Lovejoy means by realize to "physicalize—to act upon matter in such a way that the situation or configuration of things which was formerly but a dream, a hope, a purpose, takes its place among the solid, stubborn, non-contingent, public facts of the sensible world. While not the conversion of the unreal into the real, this is the conversion of a single 'essence' from one order of reality to another." [79] Therefore, an intelligent act is an act which a plan to enrich our everyday world with the merchandise from an ideal world controls; it actualizes dreams, and has them take their place among the solid facts of the sensible world.

Dewey's discussion of idea recognizes all this, says Lovejoy. It is a plan to go ahead, and as a plan is a "present as absent." It is not yet physicalized, yet has made contact with or in fact is the land that has the merchandise. Therefore the pragmatic naturalistic attempt to avoid a psychophysical dualism breaks down. The very assertion of idea or a "present as absent" is an acceptance of a psychical entity, a "content of experience which can not be assigned to the physical world as simultaneously constituted." [80] We aim at ideas which are not, at the moment they are aimed at, among the contents of the physical system, yet it is necessary to bring them before the mind as such. They stand in contrast to what we bring before the mind as already here, as given. This distinction between present and "present as absent" forces the pragmatic naturalists to acknowledge "that there is an element indispensable to the business of knowing which is not inferential but given—that there are 'present data' distinct from the 'same thing absent signified by them.' And this is all that is concerned. . . . The fact of transcendence remains; the conclusion is still inescapable that the factor in any such instance of the phenomenon called 'knowing' which is present and which 'means,' and the factor which is absent and is 'meant,' are two entities, not one." [81]

Because it seems that both sides accept "two entities, not one, in their epistemological relation, Lovejoy's objective is to assert over this undisputed fact his own interpretation of what these two entities mean. It is here that his aim to establish the *a priori* stable authority that gives the knowing process its needed structure becomes clear. His interpretation is that there is an entity of such a nature as to be able to provide the "good store of merchandise to enrich the here and now," and that there is another entity of such a nature as to be able to receive these goods. The enriching entity is a ready-made psychical existence which assumes the function of reference or of signifying, and the enriched entity is an incomplete present physical existence which can only turn to the psychical existence for its direction and completion.[82] The first is an absent object meant by the knowing experience and, therefore, is the purely immediate knowledge of a given thing. It is that to which we point, while the enriched entity is that which points. It is psychical and of a different realm from the second. Obviously Lovejoy rejects the continuity of process and object, of pointer and pointed to, and asserts that the pointed, the psychical, must direct that which points to it, the physical, as well as verify the efforts to so point. There is no possibility of true novelty on the part of the changing world, for the enriching entity, which in itself is a complete store house having no need to associate with the enriched entity, must always control its direction. It has the material to direct and verify the changing entity but it remains unchanged. Otherwise it loses its dependability.

Criticism of James' and Dewey's Concept of Truth in Process

A third way that Our Critics take to express their insistence that reality has more than flux and change or concern for the reconstruction of the practical, is to demand a separation between the object and its verification. This effort is similar to Cohen's insistence on an invariant property directing the continuity of nature and to Spaulding's insistence on an unchanging object of knowledge. Perhaps the difference is one of function. The first two dualisms drew attention to a structure that directs. This third dualism draws attention to a structure that verifies. Here the concern is with truth. Lovejoy lays the foundation for this last dualism by giving an example of a fact that exists completely within itself, transcending as a completed fact anything we might do today: "Yesterday, qûa yesterday, still remains irreducibly external to to-day, existentially transcendent of all the present thinkings and knowings which have to do with it and all the present, immediately experienced data which give circumstantial evidence concerning it." [83] Santayana carries this lead one step further and cites this completed fact as a substantial truth, as something we must consider whenever we consider this particular topic:

> If I ever find it convenient to forget my ancestors, or if my descendants find it advantageous to forget me, this fact might somewhat dash their vanity or mine if we should hear of it, but cannot touch our substantial existence or the truth of our lives. Grant this, and at once the whole universe is on its feet again, and all that strange pragmatic reduction of yesterday to tomorrow, of Sanskrit to the study of Sanskrit, of truth to the value of discovering some truth, and of matter to some human notion of matter, turns out to have been a needless equivocation, by which the perspectives of life, avowedly relative, have been treated as absolute, and the dominance of the foreground has been turned from a biological accident into a metaphysical principle.[84]

Both of these examples call for a separation between the object and its history, between the object or fact of the past and our knowledge of its today, in effect, between the criterion of truth of a proposition which lies in the past and the meaning of a proposition which may be found in the future. This separation implies that the knowledge of a fact, or the meaning of a proposition, or the history of an object concerns a past fact, or proposition, or object that is complete in itself and only awaits discovery. It is the proof that the object in fact does exist but is not that object proved.[85]

Retrospection is the "simplest, clearest, most indubitable instance" of this duality of a past object complete in itself and its verification. "While a given content of perception is 'in' consciousness, the consciousness is not then and there revealed as an element distinct from and coexistent with the content; but when that content has lapsed, a subsequent moment's experience directed back upon the former does make some kind of distinction between the previous content and the consciousness of it; and it is [in the case of perception] only from the point of view of this external reflection of present upon past that the distinction arises." [86] According to Lovejoy, this is "conclusive proof" that a duality does exist between the experience of knowing and that object known. The object to be known already exists. We must only discover it. By ignoring this distinction pragmatic naturalism "ignores the right of the object to the place it claims, a place in time prior to the date of the experience." [87]

This is of course just what the critics are afraid the pragmatic naturalist does ignore, the existence of the past event as an event logically complete in itself. The seriousness of this act of ignoring is that it seems to the critic to be a denial of objective truth. Without a past standing apart from today's and tomorrow's fluctuations and influences there is no criteria to say this or that proposition is true. The pragmatic naturalist's position is that the past, present and future form an integral continuum in which we only make distinctions for practical reasons. This continuum is all there is, and there is no objectively true reality that stands apart from this continuum measuring its validity. Rather, the continuum yields validations inasmuch as problems create its practical separations or divisions which in turn are to settle these problems. If they do, the divisions are true. In this sense we "select" truth. There is no separate complete object plus its meaning. The critic interprets this understanding of time's continuity as a confusion which sacrifices the structural real objective past to the whims of today. Pragmatic naturalistic truth identifies itself only with the settling of our own personal practical problems. It is the "well known attitude of will . . . that is concerned with its own passing caprices." [88] The metaphysical construction of such a theory of truth, and here lies its real danger, bases itself on "the assumption that the successful consequences constituting the truth of a belief must be due to the nature of the belief and not to any outside or adventitious circumstances connected with it." The result, so asserts the critic, is the rejection of truth as a universal ideal. All that is left is a relativistic, evolutionary theory "that identifies truth with those experiences of successful leading by means of which truth is sometimes verified." It is "certainly anti-realistic for it makes the *esse* of the truth relation consist in its *percipi*." [89]

Of course, the critical reaction is to deny that the personal experience of our own success in obtaining satisfaction defines truth. To assert such a thing is to deny the place of structure, meaning, purpose and being. It is insisting that all there is, is becoming, change, and flux. Just as it is vitally necessary to assert that in order to know a physical object of reference or any fact concerning it, it is necessary to know it as it really is, completely independent of the cognitive act, so it is necessary to assert that if a particular proposition is true it must "coincide with a proposition or complex entity which is found with its distinguishing characters upon it, and its consistency about it." [90] By asserting in this way that the existence of the object to be

66

known is true, the critic asserts the existence of an *a priori* realm that my knowing does not change, and that is true regardless of whether I can use it or not. In both instances this realm is completely self-sufficient and we must discover it rather than reconstruct it. The effect of this assertion is consistent with the others: novelty and open process is forbidden in order to gain *a priori* structure.

R. B. Perry makes an attempt to preserve the dynamic open aspect of pragmatic naturalism by agreeing "that truth is always related to a particular interested intention, . . . that the proof of truth must be contained within the same particular experience which manifests the intention." [91] He agrees with Woodbridge and the more sympathetic critics of pragmatic naturalism that the assertion that true knowledge must "correspond" with some *a priori* static object is taking refuge in confusion, but the vocabulary he uses in describing the truth relationships reveals a deeper kinship with the more unsympathetic critics than he may believe. He claims that truth "must envisage reality"; the object is "the element which plays the determining part in the constitution of truth; . . . truth is discovered and critically inspected experience; . . . to know is to see, whether with the bodily eye or with the eye of the soul; and that knowledge is perfected when the idea coincides with its object in direct apprehension; . . . the virtue of truth . . . is the presence of a discovered reality possessing distinction and compatible relations; . . . So far as truth is concerned, the important element of the situation is identity or consistency with reality." The essential factors in truth, "consistency as well as reality and quality, are all objective, given and not supplied. A judgment is verified when upon further inspection and confrontation with reality it stands its ground." All of these statements imply the existence of a pre-existing reality with which knowledge must agree. This example again points out that the sympathetic critic who tries to find a place within his explanation of what is ultimately significant for process, separates himself from pragmatic naturalism on exactly the same final grounds as do the other critics; that of structure. Perry, too, finally understands pragmatic naturalism as a sacrifice of ultimate structure. He cannot allow himself to accept its idea "that [the] proof, mark, or guarantee of truth is the satisfying character of that moment of the process in which the cognitive interest is fulfilled. It is this generalization which distinguishes pragmatism as a radical theory of knowledge; and it appears to me to be incorrect." [92]

Charles M. Bakewell follows almost the same procedure as does Perry. He too has a sympathetic awareness of the need for process in explaining the world and so rejects the concept of truth as "an inert static relation." Yet when he considers just what that concept does involve he finds it necessary to admit that it has "a perfectly definite, fixed, and unalterable character. When one asks for the truth regarding any situation, what he is trying to grasp is some definite relation between his ideas and experience as focussed for him in the situation he is confronting." [93]

It is even easier to quote critics who are less sympathetic with pragmatic naturalistic categories. They too demand the existence of a pre-existing structure to control and verify the continuity of everyday appearances. E. B. McGilvary declares that "sense-perception confirms the truth, but is not the truth." Rather, truth "consists in the correspondence of the images with a trans-subjective reality. . . . Truth is the agreement between ideas and reality." [94] J. Russell declares truth means "agreement or correspondence between thought and fact or reality, which is not that cognitive thought itself." In other words, we can only find truth by "a comparison between the actual and the ideal order of experience." [95] This ideal order or "reality" preserves truth from the subjectivity of appearance and gives it its characteristic of universality. The real is for all to observe. Edwin Burtt agrees, but he puts his argument the other way around and begins with our feeling that truth does have this characteristic of universality. "We feel that meaning and truth carry the implication of universality, that a certain social responsibility is bound up with them, that the reflective progress we desire is precisely in the direction of such responsibility, that in short, concepts ought to mean the same thing to all minds, and that if any statement is to be called truth it ought to be possible for any interested person to verify it as such." [96] Then he goes on to reject pragmatic naturalism because its concept of truth does not contain this universal structural aspect.

A final example is that of Josiah Royce. He develops both the concept of universality and the "ought" mentioned in Burtt's quotation above. Along with Perry and Bakewell, he admits that truth and falsity are relative to all the categories emphasized by the pragmatic naturalists; that is, insight, experience, life and action, but along with them he also will assert that behind this relativity there must be an ideal structure that stands free and clear. "Unless these constructions are what they ought to be they are not true. And unless there is an objective ought they are not even false. But if there is a true and a false, then there is a view from which the ought is known—known not as simply a single transient, unstable, chance point of view, but as the object of one self-possessed and inclusive insight such that it remains invariant whatever other points of view you attempt to conceive added to it." [97] It is this awareness of the "ought" that signifies the dualism of appearance and reality; and according to Royce we cannot ignore this awareness. He says that even the pragmatist has the inevitable conception of not only what he now needs but also of what he ought to need. Thus it is clear that not only do we have the flowing personal needs of pragmatism but we have the ideal impersonal objective needs that should direct them.

Royce uses the universal element of truth as still another substantiation of his view that there is this "ought" of a transcendental objective realm over and above the everyday realm of experience. He claims that each individual has the "need of finding companions who shall be persuaded to agree with him, or who at least ought to be persuaded." [98] This need makes explicit the universal element essential to truth for it shows that truth of necessity is beyond the individual. Truth must be above the whims of each personal subjective need. Our "need of appealing to somebody else, or to ourselves at other times, in order even to express our opinion that our judgments have a warrant, this our need for companionship is precisely coincident with our need to regard our judgment as true." [99] To believe that a judgment is true is to believe that other points of view, if these are what they ought to be, actually confirm that judgment.

CHAPTER III

PROCESS AND STRUCTURE IN THE METAPHYSICS OF WILLIAM JAMES

In the preceding chapter I have tried to point out that Our Critics have attacked pragmatic naturalism because they feel it sacrifices structure in nature to the advantage of process. In part, their understanding of the issue stems from their tendency to equate the object known and the object to be known. When the pragmatic naturalist admits that the process of knowing the object changes the object to be known, Our Critics understand this to be a denial of form or structure in the outside world and an acceptance of a world totally responsive to our desires. To some extent, all of the critics discussed in Chapter II reveal this dissatisfaction with pragmatic naturalism's attempt to explain the universe, but not all of them are critical of its fundamental attempt to introduce process into that understanding of the universe. That is, they all are dissatisfied with the place James and Dewey allot to structure but not all of them dismiss the place of process in their own understanding of the universe. In the main, those critics who think in terms of polar, natural needs are sympathetic toward a role for process in the ultimate nature of things, while those who think in terms of separate problems for the structural concern and for the process concern are unsympathetic toward a role for process in the ultimate nature of things. The former are inclined to assert that in some way man and his nature are related to the ultimately significant, whereas

71

the latter are inclined to assert a sharp separation between them.

However, on the strength of the evidence in the preceding chapter the reader should not attempt to evaluate the particular philosophical sympathies of a particular critic. The issue of their constructive philosophies is much too complicated to be covered by a survey of their critical stand toward pragmatic naturalism. For instance, Arthur O. Lovejoy, the militant critic of pragmatic naturalism, who continually argues in terms of the dualism of body and mind, also asserts that "never surely, did a sillier or more self-stultifying idea enter the human mind, than the idea that thinking as such—that is to say, remembering, planning, reasoning, forecasting—is a vast irrelevancy, having no point in the causation of man's behavior or in the shaping of his fortune." [1] What we can assert from the evidence of the preceding chapter is that Our Critics consider pragmatic naturalism to be at best incomplete, and that they all would like to insert structure as part of the nature of things. When the pragmatic naturalist attempted to give an ultimate significance to process in his consideration of nature, knowledge, and truth, Our Critics collectively asserted the existence of transcendent structures that stand over and above the flux of nature in order to control it, that stand over and above the process of knowledge in order to know and be known, and that stand over and above our processes of verification in order to give it validity. In effect Our Critics, no matter how sympathetic they are to process, saw pragmatic naturalism as a dangerous excessive assertion of this need, and therefore saw the necessity to affirm *a priori* constructions within reality which must necessarily be apart from the influence of the changes of the everyday world. These constructions must be readymade, unchanging, influential, and authoritative. Change is to uncover the unchanging and becoming is to uncover being. If the uncovering occurs, we encounter truth.

In translating these findings into the personal terms of the first chapter, it is interesting to note that the critical attack on pragmatic naturalism is in defense of the same kind of principles that the transcendent gods of law and order, i.e., El, Apollo, and God the Father, represent. These gods, and the critics' transcendent structure, represent the satisfaction of the need for separation between man's flowing world and the authoritative principles directing that flow. It is also interesting to note that pragmatic naturalism, as the critics see it, is defending the same kind of outlook on life as do the immanent gods of dynamic participation, i.e., Baal, Dionysus, and God the Son. They both represent the satisfaction of the need man has to feel that he is related to the powers of the universe and that he affects in some way nature, truth, and the object of knowledge.

There is, however, one further parallel that remains for possible development between philosophy and religion. It is that concerning a co-acceptance of the two needs. If philosophy and religion are rooted in the common endeavor to understand the whole universe, to relate various phases of experience, to find out what is ultimately significant, should not religion's final understanding of that universe as one of co-acceptance of both needs have a distinct parallel in philosophy? Must a philosophy, because it is an expression of one type of personality, sacrifice all attempts to understand that aspect of the world which answers the needs stemming from the other type of personality? It may be true that criticism of its very nature deals in either/or evaluations, for the issue here is always yes or no, a philosophy does deal successfully or does not deal successfully with what a critic thinks it should deal. But is this either/or way of looking at things necessarily true for the constructive attempts themselves? Can a philosophy attempting to understand the universe see the universe as a balance? In the terms of this book, does religion end with co-acceptance and philosophy end in antagonisms? Canaanite, Christian and

Greek religions found room for both needs despite their original tendencies. Do James and Dewey find room for both needs despite their original tendencies? The myth makers transcended their particular needs and saw their religion as essentially an expression of both types of gods. Is this true for the philosophers in this book who are the subject of criticism? Do James and Dewey transcend their particular need and attempt to find room within their understanding for an expression of both needs? Do they end in co-acceptance?

Perhaps the one assertion that can be made about William James which would be the least challenged is that he was an empiricist, and by this I simply mean he was guided by experience or experiment. For him there was need to "invoquer rien de transcendant" for "the only thing that shall be debatable among philosophers shall be things definable in terms drawn from experience." [2] James asserts that we should not understand this as a metaphysical postulate, asserting that the only thing that exists is that which we experience, but as a "methodological postulate" asserting that "nothing shall be admitted as fact . . . except what can be experienced at some definite time by some experient; and for every feature of fact ever so experienced, a definite place must be found somewhere in the final system of reality. . . . Everything real must be experienceable somewhere, and every kind of thing experienced must somewhere be real." [3] Of course he implies a metaphysic, but it is only fair to draw that implication after we understand what James meant by "experience." [4]

Another postulate, which is closely related to this methodological one, is the postulate which was to become the foundation of pragmatism:

There can be no difference anywhere that doesn't make a difference elsewhere—no difference in abstract truth that doesn't express itself in a difference in concrete fact and in conduct consequent upon that fact, imposed on somebody, somehow, somewhere, and somewhen. The whole function of philosophy ought to be to find out what definite difference it will make to you and me, at definite instants of our life, if this world formula or that world formula be the true one.[5]

That is:

The pragmatic method is primarily a method of settling metaphysical disputes that otherwise might be interminable. Is the world one or many?—fated or free?—material or spiritual? here are notions either of which may or may not hold good of the world; and disputes over such notions are unending. The pragmatic method in such cases is to try to interpret each notion by tracing its respective practical consequences. What difference would it practically make to any one if this notion rather than that notion were true? If no practical difference whatever can be traced, then the alternatives mean practically the same thing, and all dispute is idle. Whenever a dispute is serious, we ought to be able to show some practical difference that must follow from one side or the other's being right.[6]

In fact these two postulates provide the foundation for James' philosophy, the first he developed into the radical empirical theory of relations and the latter he developed into the pragmatic theory of meaning and truth. As developed doctrines, it is possible to hold one and deny the other, but as methods the two are essentially the same. The first postulate says that all facts must be experienced; the second postulate says that all differences must make a difference of fact somewhere, the first that all assertions must be experienced as facts, the second that all asserted differences must be experienced as factual differences. Each postulate starts with a cognitive assertion and each postulate traces its verification to an experienceable fact.

Because of these two postulates, James builds his philosophy upon the part, the element, the individual. He gives priority to concreteness, facts, action and power and minimizes abstractions, absolutes, *a priori* systems and fixed principles. According to him, philosophic procedure is to go from parts to wholes, treating the parts as fundamental both in the order of being and in the order of our knowledge. It must stay "inside the flux of life expectantly, recording facts, not formulating laws, and never pretending that man's relation to the totality of things as a philosopher is essentially different from his relation to the parts of things as a daily patient or agent in the practical current of events." [7] Truth lies in these recorded facts; and as they are particular facts, philosophy cannot assert final validity until all of them are recorded. "All present beliefs are subject to revision in the light of future experience." [8] Thus he stresses open air possibilities as against dogma and finality. He states that we cannot legitimately ignore any hypothesis if it actually makes a difference somewhere. It is just the incorporation of these points; that "philosophy like life must keep the doors and windows open," [9] and the associated one that allows us to keep the doors open ("we can not reject any hypothesis if consequences useful to life flow from it,") that James labels "radical empiricism":

> I say "empiricism" because it is contented to regard its most assured conclusions concerning matters of fact as hypotheses liable to modification in the course of future experience; and I say "radical," because it treats the doctrine of monism itself as an hypothesis and, unlike so much of the half-way empiricism that is current under the name of positivism or agnosticism

or scientific naturalism, it does not dogmatically affirm monism as something with which all experience has got to square.[10]

The assertion of a *radical* empiricism was necessary for James wished to distinguish his empiricism from the prevalent one that asserted that states of consciousness were synthetic products built up by the association of discrete elements. This theory was an inheritance from the British empirical tradition, particularly from Hume, who said all our perceptions are distinct existences and the mind never perceives any real connection among them. Of this James says:

Nothing could be more essentially pluralistic than the elements of Hume's philosophy. He makes events rattle against their neighbors as drily as if they were dice in a box. He might with perfect consistency have believed in real novelties, and upheld free will. But . . . most empiricists have been half hearted; and Hume was perhaps the most half hearted of the lot; in his essay "On Liberty and Necessity," he insists that the sequences which we experience, though between events absolutely disconnected, are yet absolutely uniform, and that nothing genuinely new can flow out of our lives.[11]

Hume says this uniform sequence between absolutely disconnected events is a product of habitual ways of thinking. In other words, the linkages between events are not from experience. Kant agrees with this concept of reality except that he explains the linkages or relations as due to a transcendental *a priori* synthetic factor which imposes its categories upon experience. These categories which are now necessary ways of thinking are imposed on experience from the outside. Eventually this concept of a transcendental imposer of categories develops into a doctrine of absolute Mind as the ground of the order of the world and of experience.

Most emphatically James wanted to resist this Kantian development. His object was to be more of an empiricist than Hume or Locke, not less. Kant, by his *a priori* synthetic factor, left the empirical behind. Seeking this world behind the looking glass is an "example of that Absolutism which is the great disease of philosophic thought." [12] If we take Kant's theory as a vindication of some active part played by the higher mind in the construction of experience we can accept it, but if we must accept his description of that active part, he has no place in valid philosophical development. We can much better serve philosophy by simply extending Locke's and Hume's lines.

> I believe that Kant bequeaths to us not one single conception which is both indispensable to philosophy and which philosophy either did not possess before him, or was not destined inevitably to acquire after him through the growth of men's reflection upon the hypothesis by which science interprets nature. The true line of philosophic progress lies, in short, it seems to me, not so much *through* Kant as *round* him to the point where now we stand. Philosophy can perfectly well outflank him and build herself up into adequate fulness by prolonging more directly the older English lines.[13]

He would reject the abstract creations of Kant for two empirical reasons. The first is that they can claim only a separate name as evidence for their existence. They have no place in the world of particular facts. Their being is "due to our inveterate human trick of turning names into things. . . . The low thermometer today, for instance, is supposed to come from something called the 'climate.'

78

Climate is really only the name for a certain group of days, but it is treated as if it lay behind the day, and in general we place the name, as if it were a being, behind the facts it is the name of." [14] The second is that they are useless. Their existence makes no difference anywhere. They contribute nothing to the understanding; for example:

> The Spiritualists do not deduce any of the properties of the mental life from otherwise known properties of the soul. They simply find various characters ready-made in the mental life, and these they clap into the Soul, saying, "Lo, behold the source from whence they flow." The merely verbal character of this "explanation" is obvious. The Soul invoked, far from making the phenomena more intelligible, can only be made intelligible itself by borrowing their form,—it must be represented, if at all, as a transcendent stream of consciousness duplicating the one we know. [15]

PURE EXPERIENCE

Experience

Thus James believed that it was his role in philosophy to save empiricism through greater fidelity to its source, that which is experienced. His radical empiricism was a new empiricism, a whole-hearted empiricism, proposed as a counter measure to the half-hearted empiricism of the older school. For him the order of experience, the *vera causa* of our forms of thought, our educator, our sovereign helper and our friend, is in truth a collective name for all sensible nature. Not only is it true that because experience is most intimately connected with reality, everything real must be experienced, but also everything experienced must be real. Experience is the "sole fashioner of the mind" as well as

79

the sole recorder of the mind. It is not only the experience of something foreign that impresses us, but it is the consequences of our own exertions and acts that impress us. Experience is in this sense simply a general name for whatever we think or feel. It is all that we know. We must include every end, reason, motive, object of desire or aversion, ground of sorrow or joy that we feel. "If there be real creative activities in being, radical empiricism must say, somewhere they must be immediately lived. Somewhere the *that* of efficacious causing and the *what* of it must be experienced in one, just as the what and the that of 'cold' are experienced in one whenever a man has the sensation of cold here and now." [16] Religious experience is an example of such a "creative activity" that somewhere is lived. Therefore we must include it in the total picture of reality. Its existence suggests "that our natural experience, our strictly moralistic and prudential experience may be only a fragment of real human experience." [17] Though we cannot justify its constructions, such as God, on the level of natural experience, they deserve at least a hearing on the level of this other type of experience, the emotional and moral.

The effect of broadening the concept of experience to include not only the hard irrational facts but the subjective personal facts of will, beliefs, interests, emotions, feelings, needs and intuitions, is to point out the role man plays in creating what he experiences, which in turn determines the concept of what is reality. James' rejection of the interpretation of nature as essentially disconnected elements of raw experience and his acceptance of the "felt unities" as part of reality is an example of this. Rather than considering experience as a series of distinct impacts needed to be combined by some ulterior agency, he considers experience as connections as well as terms, "journeys as well as stations." Experience does not yield qualities and terms to be related, but qualities and terms in relation.[18]

Of course, what makes the difference is the acceptance

of feeling or of consciousness as part of reality. "Realities mean . . . concrete facts, or abstract kinds of things and relations perceived intuitively between them." [19] It is true that things are discrete and discontinuous, and that "they pass before us in a train or chain, making often explosive appearances and rending each other in twain," but this coming and going is not all there is. We see them come and go, we are conscious of them flowing by us and their "coming and going . . . no more break the flow of thought that thinks them than they break the time and space in which they lie." [20] There is a coming and going but this takes place with a consciousness that sees the coming and going within a passing flow. Refusing to acknowledge the flow of consciousness is like saying a river consists of nothing but pailsful, spoonsful, quartpotsful, barrelsful of water. Even if the pails and pots were actually standing in the stream, there is more: the free water flowing between them. This is the free water of consciousness. Every definite thing in the mind is steeped and dyed in the free water that flows around it.[21]

What James means is that reality on this level consists of facts that our consciousness relates. We might label these relations that are part of experience as external relations, that is, external to the terms being related but not to the agent doing the relating. For example, the objects we experience together we tend to relate in the imagination, so that when we think of any one of them, we are likely to think of the others also, and in the same order of sequence or coexistence as before. This relation is one of mental association of empirical continuity and as such is internal to the agent experiencing the relation but external to the terms themselves. That is, these terms really are only with one another in the universe of the individual's feeling of consciousness. As a result, their relation is mutable or accidental, not constitutive nor integral to the terms related.[22]

Change, chance and free will are evidences of the

existence of these external relations. James notes that within our world, change, the relation which binds that which went before to that which is coming after, seems to be an essential ingredient. There is a history of novelties, struggles, losses and gains. As a radical empiricist he asks is not this which we witness in our own personal experience the true essential process of creation? "Is not the world really growing in these activities of ours?" [23] By asking this question he reasserts the empirical postulate that for every fact we experience we must find a definite place somewhere in the final system of reality. He notices change in his stream of consciousness and asserts that it must hold a place in ultimate reality, in pure experience.

The empirical fact of change, genuine change, involves chance. We know that the world is a really growing one; we hope that order flows from this growth. Chance becomes important here because real change or growth means that the possibilities exist that the genuine novelties produced are not what we want. This is the chance we take. But,

> let us not fear to shout it from the housetops if need be; for we now know the idea of chance is at bottom, exactly the same thing as the idea of gift,—the one simply being a disparaging, and the other a eulogistic name for anything on which we have no effective *claim*. And whether the world be the better or the worse for having either chances or gifts in it will depend altogether on what these uncertain and unclaimable things turn out to be.[24]

As further evidence of external relations, free will is necessary because it is the medium whereby we ourselves are the "authors of genuine novelty." [25] Its existence means real novelty for with it we decide between two alternatives. The proof of its existence is empirical. "Our sense of freedom supposes that some things at least are decided here and now, that the passing moment may contain some novelty, be an original starting point of events, and not merely transmit a push from elsewhere. We imagine that in some respects at least the future may not be complicated with the past, but may be really addable to it, and indeed addable in one shape or another, so that the next turn in events can at any given moment genuinely be ambiguous, i.e., possibly this, but also possibly that." [26]

James' acceptance of genuine novelties, and therefore of genuine free will, chance and change, reaffirms his basic assertion of the priority of concreteness and part as against abstractions and the whole. A reality that is truly open to the future possibilities stands in contrast to one that is ready made and complete from all eternity. Reality by being open to all possibilities is at this moment incompletely unified and perhaps may always remain so. At this moment there is no one all form or collective unit form that alone is possible. There are only individuals which we actualize in many possible ways or which we may actualize. Parts are primary and the world is "bagged piecemeal." There is no possible point of view from which the world can appear as an absolutely single fact. Wholes are simply collections, and universals are simply abstractions. The combinations that appear follow not from the inherent nature of the things but from "the order of combinations in which the elements were originally awakened by the impressions of the external world." Thus we can say "prima facie, the world is a pluralism." [27]

The Experienced

Its Flow. This world that we experience, the world of the flow of consciousness with terms in personal relation, is the primal fact upon which we work because, according to radical empiricism, it is the sole fashioner of the mind. However, in saying this we are moving from a psychological phenomenon to a metaphysic, from an understanding of a personal stream of consciousness to an objective pure experience. The only difference between the two is one of context. When we speak of our experience of continuity we are giving that continuity a central focal point and a context. When we are talking about "pure experience" we are talking about the sum total of all experience, where there is no context nor a central focal point. In this sense the discussion of reality or pure experience goes beyond the "conscious" designation. Reality is "a that, an absolute, a pure experience on an enormous scale, undifferentiated and undifferentiable, into thought and thing." [28] This objective world of real relations neutralizes all distinctions. "Pure experience" denotes a form of being which is as yet neutral or ambiguous, and prior to object and subject distinctions. It is prior to the distinction between physical facts and felt continuities. "Thought and things are absolutely homogeneous as to their material, and . . . their opposition is only one of relation and of function. There is no stuff different from thing stuff, . . . but the same identical pieces of 'pure experience' [which was the name I gave to the *materia prima* of everything] [which] can stand alternately for a 'fact of consciousness' or for a physical reality, according as it is taken in one context or in another." [29] It is prior to all cognition as well as to physical traits. It thereby furnishes the material for our later reflection. "It is plain, unqualified activity, or existence, a simple *that*. In this *naif* immediacy it is of course valid; it is there, we act upon it; and the doubling of it in retrospection into a state of mind and a reality intended thereby, is just one of the acts. . . . The immediate experience in its passing is always 'truth,' practical truth, *something to act on,* at its own movement. If the world were then and there to go out like a candle it would remain truth absolute and objective and no one would ever oppose the thought in it to the reality intended." [30]

Another revealing but difficult to understand characteristic of pure experience is its "much at onceness" that transcends all separation. As such it is similar to the impression made on the conscious level if a number of impressions, from any number of sensory sources, fall simultaneously on a mind which had not yet experienced them separately. Such a mind would fuse them into a single undivided object. In this case, and in that of pure experience there is no meaning, only a "big blooming buzzing confusion." But in another sense, there is meaning because all there is in each case is pure experience. Things are what they are experienced as, but the word experience here designates pure experience. As we contact them on our stream of consciousness level they have some meaning but on the level of pure experience they mean everything they are. On that level things compenetrate each other, are alive and fuse into each other, thus figuring in different constellations and different streams of consciousness without ceasing to be themselves. Therefore the thing about which we think belongs to two different continuums, that of consciousness and that of pure experience. In the former it is a discriminated part, meaning one thing, in the latter an unbroken unit, a much at onceness, meaning everything.[31]

In order to understand what James means by his doctrine of compenetration it might be well to compare it to mosaic artwork. In actual mosaics the individual pieces are held together by their bedding, "for which bedding the Substances, transcendental Egos, or Absolutes of other philosophies may be taken to stand." James' radical empiricism removes the bedding and the pieces cling together just by their edges with the experienced relations forming their cement. Now with the doctrine of compenetration the stress is on the point that the mosaic pieces run into each other continuously. There is "in general no separateness needing to be overcome by an external cement." [32] Every individual morsel of the sensational stream takes up its adjacent morsels by coalescing with them. The relations experienced between terms or facts on the conscious level are now immediately conscious of continuing in each other on the pure experience level. For instance, the organization of the Self as a system of facts, memories, purposes, strivings, fulfilments or disappointments, on the conscious level is superficially expressing the most intimate of all relations, on the pure experience level that of suffusion and compenetration of the whole. Perhaps the term "dynamic connection" expresses this intimate relation because in this case a thing only has being as it enters into the being of other things and yet enters in a flowing continuous way.[33]

Its Structure. James' whole endeavor is to assert that reality, pure experience, and the field of consciousness are one and the same. Toward this end he advances the doctrine of compenetration to explain the felt unities of consciousness as it exists in pure experience. But he is also compelled to explain separation, for within the realm of consciousness there are not only relations but also separation. Separateness is actually experienced and it stays and counts as separateness to the end.

> Grant for example that our human subjectivity determines what we shall say things are; grant that it gives the "predicates" to all the "subjects" of our conversation. Still the fact remains that some subjects are there for us to talk about, and others not there; and the further fact that, in spite of so many different ways in which we may perform the talking, there still is a grain in the subjects which we can't well go against, a cleavage-structure which resists certain of our predicates and makes others slide in more easily. Does not this stubborn that of some things and not of others; does not this imperfect plasticity of them to

our conceptual manipulation, oppose a positive limit to the sphere of influence of humanistic explanation? [34]

Earlier, I hinted at the explanation of how ultimate reality, or pure experience, can contain dynamic flowing change as well as these structural separations when I said that things compenetrate each other, are alive and fuse with each other yet *never cease to be themselves*. Compenetration does not mean complete merging of every bit of experience with every other bit, but there is a sort of continuity where the threads of compenetration extend only for a limited distance and one part of the "muchness" is only indirectly connected with its remoter part. Reality is a scene of perpetual transition in which the parts inherit one another and usher one another in. No event expires until after another has already begun, so that there is always a continuous zone of commingled dawn and twilight through which the one leads to the other. But at the same time each object only extends for a limited distance.[35] This allows pure experience which antedates our personal subjective experience to possess in its own right a concatenated or continuous structure which lends itself only partly to our translations of consciousness. We on the conscious level form things and relate them; but reality, pure experience, is in no wise constrained to "back" the personal subjective relation. If it does back it, the personal relation of consciousness is true.[36] It then so to speak possessed the true subjective formation virtually or potentially.

In effect, what James is asserting is that pure experience not only is full of relations, corresponding to the relations of the stream of consciousness, but that it resists some relations, corresponding to the separation experienced in the stream of consciousness. In other words, reality has discontinuities as well as continuities. In certain situations it actually speaks for itself, resisting some lines of attack on our part and opening itself to others. "The law is that all things fuse that can fuse, and nothing separates except what must." [37] Thus we do not only form reality, but at times it directs us according to its inbuilt structure, its own unities. These we must note down and use. Our relations, our mental network, flung over pure experience will fail if instead of choosing conductors for its work we choose non-conductors. We must recognize that reality has its tendencies, its pathways, its resistances, its desires, its directions, its mechanical conditions and its kinds.[38] All of these we must take into consideration. Our results depend upon it. "What makes the assumption 'scientific' and not merely poetic, what makes a Helmoltz and his kin discoverers, is that the things of Nature turn out to act as if they were of the kind assumed." [39] Reality of itself comes in coherent forms, in *a priori* conjunctions that scientific assumptions must accept. The acceptance of these pathways, these *a priori* conjunctions, is the acceptance of inner relations.

> The second part of reality, as something that our beliefs must also obediently take account of . . . falls into two sub-parts: 1) the relations that are mutable and accidental, as those of date and place; and 2) those that are fixed and essential because they are grounded on the inner natures of their terms. Both sorts of relation are matters of immediate perception. Both are "facts." But it is the latter kind of fact that forms the more important sub-part of reality for our theories of knowledge. Inner relations namely are "eternal," are perceived whenever their sensible terms are compared; and of them our thought— mathematic and logical thought so-called—must eternally take account.[40]

This assertion that these eternal inner relations present irreducible data which form a system, a structure, that we write down, is important because it means that James is not asserting a purely subjective concept of nature that is subject to our everyday whims. Pure experience is neutral to whatever divisions the flow of consciousness may give it, but it does contain potencies to certain distinctions and divisions and not to others. Thus the only conclusion possible is that there is a minimum of structure in pure experience that the contributing subjective aspects of the stream of consciousness must recognize.[41] James may resist this and speak at times of a first as structureless and then of a second which gives structure, but even in these passages the duality isn't complete for the conscious mind, the second, has no interest in legislating structure for all possible experience. Rather, it is interested in subjective fact and hopes to discover outer realities over which its ideal network may be flung so that its ideal and the real may coincide. In fact this is the general objective of scientific and philosophic thought: to make the two orders, that of nature and that of consciousness, coincide. So far as we do this "we can make *a priori* propositions concerning natural fact."[42]

METHOD

What I have said so far is that James believes that we can reach an understanding of ultimate reality, pure experience, by observing the field of consciousness. Because consciousness presents itself in a continuous flux with facts in relation, so pure experience must consist of a continuity with things distinct within the flow. This distinction within the flow suggests that ultimate reality itself has a structure that we must recognize in a functional sense. In other words, there is not an ultimate reality first built up in a static completed form which we must discover, but there is a certain neutral flow containing its own functional tendencies and resistances. When we impose our present

89

distinction on pure experience for specific functional purposes or uses, we must take into account this "cleavage structure which resists certain of our predicates and makes others slide in more easily." [43] To the extent that we recognize this "cleavage structure," to that extent it is unfair to consider James' pragmatism as a pure process philosophy which ignores structure. An example of a functional imposition upon pure experience is the flow of consciousness. Pure experience and the stream of consciousness are the same entity or the same stuff, but they are also different because of the personal aspect. The plenum of pure experience comes to us "as a chaos of fragmentary impressions interrupting each other." [44] Pure experience is pure experience whereas the stream of consciousness is known pure experience: thus the difference. The moment we know it, it is no longer a much at onceness but "a mass of present sensation in a cloud of memories, emotions, concepts, etc." [45] This mass of present sensation is a selection from pure experience for a purpose and so consciousness is a function rather than an entity. It is a function to serve its purpose, but to fulfill this service consciousness must first know pure experience. Consciousness is the function of knowing pure experience.[46]

James identifies perception and conception as ways for the consciousness to know pure experience but he draws on percepts as the more revealing because only here is the moving real world of pure experience, the world of causal and dynamic relations, of activity and history, really caught.[47] Reality only opens itself to the sympathetic apprehension of immediate feeling, of immediate concrete perception, because in the perceptual experience we get "intension" rather than "extension." Only in perception "do we acquaint ourselves with continuity, or the immersion of one thing in another, . . . with self, with substance, with qualities, with activity in its various modes, with time, with cause, with change, with novelty, with tendency, and with freedom." [48] Radical empiricism, by insisting on this priority of percepts, yet realizing they are as much functional artifacts as any concept, holds on to this life flow. It reasserts the existence of transitions and vitality in the truly real.[49]

Because perceptions have the ability to grasp connections as well as divisions, they are not distinct in the sense of being sharply sundered and mutually exclusive; rather, they overlap and lead into one another. Understood as such, they are related to such expressions as sensation, feeling, intuition, sensible experience and immediate flow of conscious life. The good thing about this is that they capture the flow of reality; the bad thing is they get "each successive moment of experience, as the sessile sea-anemone on its rock receives whatever nourishment the wash of the waves bring." [50] We humans are more than passive sea-anemone, however. We must, therefore, form concepts in order to deal more effectively with the future, to further the ends of our life. We form concepts in order to prepare for what might be ahead, "so that on the whole we may prosper and our days be long in the land." [51] "The environment kills as well as sustains us, and . . . the tendency of raw experience to extinguish the experient himself is lessened just in the degree in which the elements in it that have a practical bearing upon life are analyzed out of the continuum and verbally fixed and coupled together, so that we may know what is in the wind for us and get ready to react in time." [52] In other words, our concepts are examples of our imposing functional uses on to the flow of neutrality within the already functional imposition of the flow of consciousness. Its job is to summarize old facts and lead us on to new ones. We reduce the complex experience to manipulable selectivity that we can use for getting about our already selective sensible experience.

This is the important point to remember in understanding James' place for conceptual knowledge or the intellectual life as he sometimes calls it. This is an activity consisting almost wholly of a substitution "of a conceptual order for the perceptual order in which experience originally comes." [53] It is a secondary process, that presupposes perception, which is not indispensable to life, and which we employ because it is useful. It contains nothing of any higher nature which the concrete perceptive descriptions have left out, being only "a man-made language, a conceptual shorthand . . . in which we write our reports of nature." [54] It is man made because we pick out and identify a numerically distinct and permanent subject of discourse. It is our handling of sensible experience; it is our grasping of a fleeting moment of reality and labeling it, conceptualizing it. Concepts give the aboriginal flow of feeling halting places. We form them much in the same way that "a man by looking through a tube may limit his attention to one part after another of a landscape." But this selective grasp of reality is not insulation. It no more breaks reality than the "tube breaks the landscape. Concepts are notes, views, taken on reality not pieces of it, as bricks are of a house." [55] There is no substantive impression of it standing out by itself. Concepts are man made.

If we now direct our attention to the purpose of concepts rather than to what they are, it is possible to say that they do add to reality. Conception is a faculty superadded to our perceptual consciousness and used for a purpose. "We harness perceptual reality in concepts in order to drive it better to our ends." [56] There is perceptual reality plus our harness. It is a form superimposed for practical ends. This is what James means when he says that "the pure sciences form a body of propositions with whose genesis experience has nothing to do." [57] These sciences of classification, logic and mathematics for instance, are products of a conceptual knowledge twice removed from pure experience. Their concepts are harnesses of reality but they must never be taken as the full equivalent of reality. Not only because the concept is the selected part of reality but also because its nature is

92

static and discontinuous while reality is dynamic and flowing. Each concept means just what it singly means, and nothing else. "Conceptions form the one class of entities that cannot under any circumstances change. They can cease to be altogether; or they can stay as what they severally are; but there is for them no middle way. They form an essentially discontinuous system, and translate the process of our perceptual experience, which is naturally a flux into a set of stagnant and petrified terms. The very conception of flux itself is an absolutely changeless meaning in the mind: it signifies just that one thing, flux, unmovably." [58] Thus "every smallest state of consciousness, concretely taken, overflows its own definition." [59] For instance, the concept change has no change in it. The stages into which we analyze change are states with the change itself going on in between. It lies along the interval, inhabiting what the definition fails to gather up. Change overflows its definition in other words. Concepts can name change and growth but are not capable of translating them into terms of their own. They can give us only a bare abstract outline or approximate sketch of the universe. The essential features of the flux always escape whenever we substitute the conceptual order for the perceptual order.

EFFECT

The effect of this whole emphasis on percepts as reaching into pure experience and concepts as extensive weapons of the mind using this pure experience is both negative and positive. James believes the negative effect is that it saves him from the rationalistic (or the absolutistic—for they are related in that they each represent the world as "unchanging, eternal, or out of time,") sin of "vicious abstractionism." He defines this as the giving to the concept an existence of its own prior to that from which it really stems, or the "taking the mere name and nature of a fact and clapping it behind the fact as a duplicate entity to make it possible." [60] It is a product of the tendency toward security, the tendency to treat the stable conceptions as the more essential thing in knowledge, to believe sincerely "that the intelligible order ought to supersede the senses rather than interpret them." [61] This tendency (James would rather call it Transcendentalistic than Rationalistic because he prefers the contrasting label Empirical to Irrationalistic) thinks of conceptual knowledge not only as the more noble knowledge but as knowledge originating independently of all perceptual particulars. Concepts follow from the very nature of the elements themselves and therefore no amount of experience can modify them. The resulting tendency is to emphasize abstraction and also to make wholes prior to parts, in the order of knowledge and in the order of being.

The positive effect of James' empirical emphasis on the primacy of percepts is that it allows him to understand the total picture of reality, the non-rational as well as the rational. Everything that we experience is given equal status with everything else. We experience continuity and flow and so we accept them. Rational or transcendental attempts to conceive of reality in terms of concepts only "draws the dynamic continuity out of nature as you draw the thread out of a string of beads." [62] In fact if this "continuity and flow mean logical self contradiction, the logic must go." [63] The important thing is to be fair to the totality, the irrational as well as the rational. Pure experience transcends all of these distinctions so we must consider the total when we develop a philosophy of nature or of pure experience. We must consider our needs, our likes, our dislikes, as well as our thoughts and our mind. All of these human capacities have a place in pure experience so they all must be ultimate factors in a philosophy. Rational philosophy does try to answer to our liking for disinterested love of information, the love of consistency in thought, philosophic contemplation, the ideal fealty of Truth (with a capital T), the drive to reduce the manifold in thought to simple form, but it tends to ignore the human capacities for social affections, play, intimations of art, religious emotion, moral self-approbation, fancy and wit, as well as the human capacity for faith (the capacity to believe on incomplete evidence and to act on such belief).

James accounts for the expression of the subjective element, or the non-rational if you prefer, in his development of the meaning of the concept. First there is a brute existential pure experience which marks the limit of rationality, the limit of conceptualizing. However, a part of that brute fact is our needs and our interests, and that to which we attend and make emphatic within pure experience is up to us. As we lay the emphasis here or there, quite different streams of consciousness result. We read the facts differently. What we say about reality depends on the perspective into which we throw it. We break the flux of sensible reality into things at our will, at our desire. We create the subjects and the predicates of our true as well as of our false propositions. The flux is there, but what we "see" depends upon us. Reality is disproportionate to the way it grasps us, and our interests determine this. "Out of the aboriginal sensible muchness our attention carves out objects, which conception then names and identifies forever—in the sky 'constellations,' on the earth 'beach,' 'sea,' 'cliff,' 'bushes,' 'grass.' Out of time we cut 'days' and 'nights,' 'summers' and 'winters.' We say what each part of the sensible continuum is, and all these abstracted whats are concepts." [64] Thus the concept is nothing but a manner of attending to certain objects, or consenting to their stable presence before the mind. Of course the concept is subject to the structure of reality, but barring this limitation on its constructive powers the mind can carry on its conceptualizing or analyzing to any extent it cares. Conceptual knowledge thus depends upon us. For instance,

The most persistent outer relations which science believes in are never matters of experience at all, but have to be disengaged from under experience by a process of elimination, that is, by ignoring conditions which are always present. The elementary laws of mechanics, physics, and chemistry are all of this sort. The principle of uniformity in nature is of this sort; it has to be sought under and in spite of the most rebellious appearances; and our conviction of its truth is far more like a religious faith than like assent to a demonstration.[65]

In this sense reality is responsive to human needs and interests, without which things are not. "The knower is an actor and co-efficient of the truth on one side, whilst on the other he registers the truth which he helps to create. Mental interests, hypotheses, postulates, so far as they are bases for human action—action which to a great extent transforms the world—help to make the truth which they declare. In other words, there belongs to mind, from its birth upward, a spontaneity, a vote. It is in the game, and not a mere looker on. . . ."[66] And these needs that the human brings to the knowing situation are *a priori* to that situation. All our minds' contents are alike empirical, but the emphasis and accentuation is *a priori*. Interests we bring with us and simply posit or take our stand upon them.

This point is vitally important. It is the culmination of James' thought. It is revolutionary for it associates what is with the process recognizing it. James is making the unbelievable assertion that "le monde sera que ce que nous le ferons."[67] We must use our mental activity or else objects known will be different. Mental process is a vital living activity that actually creates on the basis of interests and needs. It is subject to the stream of pure experience, but the mind is a teleological instrument that reaches out and draws from pure experience what it prefers. The resultant world "dipped out from the stream of time," is ours. "We plunge forward into the field of fresh experience with the beliefs our ancestors and we have made already; these determine what we notice; what we notice determines what we do; what we do again determines what we experience; so from one thing to another, although the stubborn fact remains that there is a sensible flux, what is true of it seems from first to last to be largely a matter of our own creation." [68] Millions of items of the outward order are present to our senses which never properly enter into our experience because they have no interest for us. "My experience is what I agree to attend to. Only those items which I notice shape my mind." [69] "This whole function of conceiving, of fixing, and holding fast to meanings, has no significance apart from the fact that the conceiver is a creature with a partial purpose and private ends." [70] All classifications, categories, and essences are products of private ends. Their names signify properties of a thing which are so important for an individual's interests that in comparison with it he neglects the rest. "The mind, in short, works on the data it receives very much as a sculptor works on his block of stone. In a sense the statue stood there from eternity. But there were a thousand different ones beside it and the sculptor alone is to thank for having extricated this one from the rest." [71]

TRUTH

I have presented James' metaphysic, or his philosophy of nature, and in a sense I have finished the chapter. He *does* find a place for structure and *does* recognize that both process and structure have a place in pure experience. However, in another sense, the empirical sense, the most important part of the chapter still remains, that of presenting the entire philosophy in a concrete working system and making explicit its implications. James does this for us in his discussion on truth.[72] Here structure as well as process is important.

The attempt to explain just what truth is, is especially important to James because of his stress on a metaphysics of flux and on empirical procedure. It seemed to him that almost all previous scientific and philosophical thought has supposed that "Truth" consisted of a hard and fast system of propositions, eternally valid in themselves, which our minds had only to copy literally. Without thinking, scientists and philosophers alike assumed that truth was the simple duplication by the mind of this ready made and given reality. In such a system truth means an inert, static relation. "When you've got your true idea of anything, there's an end of the matter—You're in possession; you know; you have fulfilled your thinking destiny. . . . Epistemologically you are in stable equilibrium." [73] James describes this truth that is true even if no one discovers it, to be "like the coat that fits though no one has ever tried it on, like the music that no ear has listened to." [74]

This *a priori* stand concerning truth opposes everything James has taught. For one thing, there is simply no empirical test available for adjudicating between divers types of thoughts which claim to be in communication with the "ready made and given reality. . . . Common sense, common science or corpuscular philosophy, ultra-critical science, or energetics, and critical or idealistic philosophy, all seem insufficiently true in some regard and leave some dissatisfaction." [75] For another, there are empirical influences that have actually helped to dissolve away this appearance of absoluteness in the facts and truths that we formulate:

First, philosophic criticisms like those of Mill, Lotze, and Sigwart have emphasized the incongruence of the forms of our thinking with the "things" which the thinking nevertheless successfully handles (Predicates and subjects, for example, do not live separately in the things, as they do in our judgments of them). Second, not only has the doctrine of Evolution weaned us from fixities and inflexibilities in general, and given us a world all plastic but it has made us ready to imagine almost all our functions, even the intellectual ones, as "adaptations," and possibly transient adaptations, to practical human needs. Lastly, the enormous growth of the sciences in the past fifty years has reconciled us to the idea that "Not quite true" is as near as we can ever get.[76]

Empirically, then, truth is not this search for the absolute that transcends the everyday realm of change but it is involved in change, accepting it yet using it in conjunction with our aspirations. Truth understood in this way is "the opposite of whatever is stable, of whatever is practically disappointing, of whatever is useless, of whatever is lying and unreliable, of whatever is unverifiable and unsupported, of whatever is inconsistent and contradictory, of whatever is artificial and egocentric, of whatever is unreal in the sense of being of no practical account." [77] It is what we say about reality rather than reality itself. If what we say comes into fruition, it is true. Truth is intrinsically related to what we say, to our knowledge or to our opinions and beliefs, but what we say is not true until pure experience ultimately agrees with it or verifies it.

Because James stresses verification as well as the idea of what we say, about reality, it might be fairer to say that truth is the relation between the idea and the reality than to say it is the idea itself. Truth is something about the idea, a property of the idea, an attribute of the idea; better yet, the success of the idea, or the working of the idea. This "something about an idea" is its workableness, our ability to verify it, to work up to an object or an intended objective. First there is an idea. It does not immediately obtain its objective but only works from next to next so as to reach it eventually. If it does reach it finally, we can call this idea a true one. If it seems to be able to reach its object eventually, we might still consider it as possessing "trueness." If it fails to reach it, there is no relation, no verification, *ipso facto* there is only fact. We are no longer dealing with truth.[78]

Truth then is a relation between an idea and a reality outside of the idea. It is the circumstance surrounding the object and the idea about the object which we can either short circuit or traverse at full length. So long as it exists and a satisfactory passage through it between the object and the idea is possible, that idea is true whether fully developed passage takes place or not. The point is, passage or verification must be possible. The idea must actually make possible a "pointing," "fitting," "corresponding," "adapting," or "agreeing" with or to the object. In this sense truth means the idea is in agreement with reality, the idea points to the reality, an idea's truth has the power to adapt us to a reality, our ideas fit reality. These terms all express the mediating train of verification which makes the idea true.

So far, what I have emphasized in this discussion on truth is that aspect which looks to something else for final verification. This makes it clear that it is unfair to say that James is giving unbridled leeway to any idea that might come into his head. He defines truth as the relation between an idea and a reality outside of the idea. Thus the idea must confront "facts." One may think ever so clearly and ever so necessarily but this will prove nothing, unless there exists the crucial evidence, the testimony of the "facts" themselves. For the idea struggling to obtain truth this is a confrontation with an objective reality because it is "a standing reality independent of the idea that knows it," which "opinions must acknowledge in order to be true." [79] But we must remember that this objective reality or "facts" that an idea must acknowledge does not stand apart from pure experience or the observer. It transcends the particular situational idea but does not transcend all experience. Its existence is proof that there is more than the feelings of the moment, and therefore serves as a check on them. It is proof that ideas are subject to the structure of pure existence. But this check, or in Santayana's phrase, background, is "nothing more than the other . . . experience with which a given present experience may find itself in point of fact mixed up." [80] James begins with a reality but it is a reality abstracted from pure experience. There is "no good warrant for even suspecting the existence of any reality of a higher denomination than that distributed and strung-along and flowing sort of reality which we finite beings swim in. That is the sort of reality given us." [81]

This emphasis on the retrospective aspect of truth, that part of truth that must acknowledge the structure of pure experience, isn't by any means the whole picture, nor in fact the major portion of the picture as James sees it. It is true the object of an idea must be in line with certain affinities or potencies of pure experience, and in this sense we find it, but it is also true that we are responsible for the idea that points, that creates it. The object is ours so to speak. When our concern is focused on this aspect of the truth relationship it becomes prospective and a new vocabulary is applicable, one distinctly emphasizing the functional relationship of ends and purposes. "The truth of a thing or idea is its meaning, or its destiny, that which grows out of it." [82] Achievements and prospects cognitively justify ideas. The past does not vouch for the truth, rather the future verifies it. No doubt the *a priori* internal structure of reality plays a role in truth, but as far as cognition is concerned, the important thing is that which comes after and which decides the issue of truth or falsity. Every idea or cognitive project is on trial, and is bound to submit itself to the fresh findings of the future. Truth is the relation between the idea and reality, but that reality is ultimately a perceptual flux open to change. It is this looking ahead

101

to the future that helps to save James from a static concept of truth. A true idea must agree with reality or with a definite object but that reality is open to being worked or led. The truth of an idea is its workings or that in it which by ordinary psychological law sets up those workings.[83]

When we understand truth as the workings of an idea and emphasize that it is our idea and our workings, and in fact our object, that comes into actuality, we understand truth as our addition to reality. That which is additive are human needs or interests. It is as if we liken the world to a cast of beans onto a table.

> By themselves they spell nothing. An onlooker may group them as he likes. He may simply count them all and map them. He may select groups and name these capriciously, or name them to suit certain extrinsic purposes of his. Whatever he does, so long as he *takes account* of them, his account is neither false nor irrelevant. If neither, why not call it true. It *fits* the beans-*minus*-him, and expresses the *total* fact or beans-*plus*-him. Truth in this total sense is partially ambiguous, then. If he simply counts or maps, he obeys a subjective interest as much as if he traces figures. Let that stand for pure "intellectual" treatment of the beans, while grouping them variously stands for non-intellectual interests. All that Schiller and I contend for is that there is *no* "truth" without *some* interest, and that non-intellectual interests play a part as well as intellectual ones.[84]

Interest and needs create truth, effect reality. "Reality is an accumulation of our own intellectual inventions, and the struggle for 'truth' in our progressive dealings with it is always a struggle to work in new nouns and adjectives while altering as little as possible the old." [85]

Our efforts to satisfy our needs and interests by securing

for them a reality in the flow of consciousness is both inten-
tional and unintentional. Often, we automatically act on our
needs and interests but at other times we first will that we
shall listen to our needs and interests, and then act on that
will. These actions can really effect, really count, really
construct, really determine what is. Actions based on will
really can make truth. Those ideas that will takes hold
of become preferred forms of life, something to be made
real through the energy of that will. If we have our way, our
ideal is more than a bare abstract possibility, it becomes an
actual thing, thus expressing the flow of ultimate reality:
the ideal and the real are dynamically continuous. But this
passage from an ideal to a reality in the flow of consciousness can only take place if we thoroughly believe in the
idea. With this we come back again to human needs and
desires, for we believe in that which is in line with our
needs.[86]

In considering when it is proper for the will and belief
to work in conjunction, James gives two answers. The first
is when abstinence from belief or suspension of judgment
means losing the chance of truth. We have the right and
the duty to believe at our own risk any hypothesis that is
live enough to tempt our will, that has some degree of
vital heat for us, although such belief must not be inconsistent with the facts. We assume here the belief that we in
fact do have freedom to believe and create, and that
abstinence or suspension of judgment is equivalent to a
disbelief when sensible facts are noncommittal, when the
intellect of the individual cannot by itself resolve the living
option. James feels that to preach skepticism as a duty
until we find sufficient evidence is tantamount to saying
that to yield to our fear of being in error is wise and better
than to yield to our hope that a particular desire is true.
The issue is not skepticism and the intellect against a faith
decision and passion but passion against passion: fear of
being in error against hope of being true.

. . . we must now bow to the necessity of making a choice; for suspense itself would be a choice, and a most practical one, since by it we should forfeit the possible benefits of boldly espousing a possible truth. If this *be* a moral world, there are cases in which any indecision about its being so must be death to the soul. Now, if our choice is predetermined, there is an end of the matter; whether predetermined to the truth or fatality or the delusion of liberty, is all one for us. But if our choice is truly free, then the only possible way of getting at that truth is by the exercise of the freedom which it implies. Here, the act of belief and the object of belief coalesce, and the very essential logic of the situation demands that we wait not for any outward sign, but, with the possibility of doubting open to us, voluntarily take the alternative of faith. Renouvier boldly avows the full conditions under which alone we can be right if freedom is true, and says: "Let our liberty pronounce on its own real existence." It as a necessity being alike indemonstrable by any quasimaterial process, must be postulated if taken at all.[87]

The second answer to the question as to when it is proper to act in order to actualize an ideal is related to the first but emphasizes the future. We have the right to believe when the effect of conviction can bring about the very facts in which we believe. This holds true of all beliefs regarding the future when that future depends in some measure on the will. Suppose:

Je me trouve dans un mauvais pas dont je ne peux sortir que par un saut hardi et dangereus, et ce saut, je voudrais le pouvoir faire, mais j'ignore, faute d'expérience, si j'en aurai la force. Supposons que j'emploie la méthode subjective: je crois ce que je desire ma confiance me donne des forces et rend possible ce qui, sans elle, ne l'êut peut-être pas été. Je franchis donc l'espace et me voilà hors de danger. Mais supposons que je sois disposè a nier ma capacité, par ce motif qu'elle ne m'a pas encore été demontree par ce genre d'exploits: alors je balance j'hesite, et tant et tant qu'a la fin, affaibli et tremblant, réduit, à prendre un elan de pur désespoir, je manque mon coup et je tombe dans l'abîme. En pareil cas, quoi qu'il en puisse advenir, je ne serai qu'un sot se je ne crois pas ce que je desire, car ma croyance se trouve être une condition préliminaire, indispensable de l'accomplissement de son objet qu'elle affirme. Croyant a mes forces je m'elance; le resultat donne raison à ma croyance, la verifee; c'est alors seulement qu'elle de vient vraie, mais alors on peut dire aussi qu'elle etait vraie. Il y a donc des cas ou une croyance cree sa propre vérification. Ne croyez pas vous aurez raison; et, en effet, vous tomberez dans l'abîme. Croyez, vous aurez enclore raison, car vous vour sauverez. Tout la difference entre les deuz cas, c'est que le second vous est fort advantageux.[88]

James' own personal example is his affirmation of free will. He assumes that in fact we do have free will.[89]

James' instrumentalism is evident. The acceptance of a belief, i.e., free will, is not advanced so as to be an answer to an enigma in which we can rest, in which we can fall back upon, but it is an instrument with which we move forward and make over nature.[90] Without these beliefs reality as a whole appears incomplete. Yet nature has its own inbuilt limitation to this instrumental aspect of belief. We have the right to believe what we can effect by that belief, but everything hinges on the bringing about of the desired consequences. The procedure starts with the will applying itself in the form of attention to ideas. Then, when these attended ideas survive to the exclusion of others, they must express themselves in appropriate action. If all goes well, the needs and interests of the individual which stimulated the will in the first place reach a satisfactory consequence, that is, they now have a place in the total flow of conscious reality. The steps are:

1. There is nothing absurd in a certain view of the world being true, nothing self-contradictory;
2. It *might* have been true under certain conditions;
3. It *may* be true, even now;
4. It is *fit* to be true;
5. It *ought* to be true;
6. It *must* be true;
7. It *shall* be true, at any rate true for me.[91]

This is not an intellectual chain of inference but rather a slope of good will in which the "it shall be true" consequence represents a consequence of a satisfaction of our needs and interests. The good consequence is not a sign or mark of truth's presence but is the *cause existendi* of the belief that started the "slope."

Again, the dynamic aspect of needs and interests is evident. The idea in which we believe struggles to work in its character of what reality should be. It is true if it succeeds and works to "some sensible terminus or other that can be verified exactly." [92] "The chain of workings which an opinion sets up is the opinion's truth, falsehood, or irrelevancy, as the case may be. Every idea that a man has works some consequences in him, in the shape either of bodily actions or of other ideas. Through these consequences the man's relations to surrounding realities are modified. He is carried nearer to some of them and further from others, and gets now the feeling that the idea has worked satisfactorily, now that it has not. The idea has put him into touch with something that fulfills its intent, or it has not." [93] We cannot define truth without referring to this functional follow up of action. The possession of true thought means the possession of invaluable instruments of action. In fact, truth is only the expedient in the way of our thinking. Truth is an aid in a world of flowing reality, it is a "guiding thread by which man finds his way and keeps his footing in the midst of perceptual novelty. Truth is a route which man takes in traversing nature." [94] Our actions make it; it can only exist in act. It energizes and does battle, not only by liberating and setting free more experience but by limiting, defining and adjusting to definite ends. If the battle guides and gets us there, it is true. The working, the action, the leading must reach an outcome, an upshoot, a *terminus ad quem,* this is the verification, the consequence that makes action true. The "only test of probable truth is what works best in the way of leading us," leading us to what essentially we create by our needs and interests.[95]

There remains one last question to answer in regard to James' pragmatic concept of truth. That is, what difference does it make if I believe something to be true? James defines truth as "essentially a relation between two things, an idea, on the one hand, and a reality outside of the idea, on the other." But because the pragmatic method insists that there is no difference of truth that does not make a difference of fact somewhere, we must seek to determine the meaning of all differences of opinion by making the discussion hinge as soon as possible upon some practical or particular issue. If it is true that "the effective meaning of any philosophic proposition can always be brought down to some particular consequences in our future practical experience," [96] then the truth relation must have "its fundamentum, namely the matrix of experiential circumstances, psychological as well as physical, in which the correlated terms are found embedded." [97] An idea is only true when we convert it into perceptual experience. Beliefs must show consequences in order to be true and these consequences must never stay aloft in the mental conceptual realm. They must redescend to the purer or more concrete level again. Put pragmatically, the question now is: "How is the world made different for me by my conceiving an opinion of mine under the concept true?" Or, "grant an idea or belief to be true . . . what concrete difference will its being true make in anyone's actual life. What in short is the truth's cash value in experiential terms?" [98]

To find the answer to this question we must introduce "satisfaction" into our emphasis on the prospective verification of the true. This is because a major aspect of truth lies in mental consequences. Previously we said that truth is a process of verifying itself. Events that follow its declaration make it happen to an idea. "Truth *happens* to an idea. It *becomes* true, is *made* true by events." [99] If this is so, how can we recognize particularly successful mental events? The answer is to introduce the new mental element of satisfaction. "Like Dewey and Schiller, I have had to say the truth of an idea is determined by its satisfactoriness." [100]

However, we must not consider this element apart from other consequences of other true beliefs. Even when we are emphasizing the prospective direction of truth we must take into account the structure of pure experience. The satisfaction or fact to which our idea leads does not take place in a vacuum. The reality created by the ideal must be in harmony with pure experience and other realities created previously. We must marry previous parts of experience and reality with the newer parts we want to be true. "To be true means only to perform this marriage function." [101] In other words, our satisfactions and our facts must be in accord with the rest of reality. The greatest enemy to any one of our truths is our other truths. This means "all present beliefs are subject to revision in the light of future experiences." [102] It means we must assimilate, validate and verify such beliefs. The introduction of satisfactoriness just adds up to this: the richest fit is the truest fit. The truest scientific hypothesis is that which works to bring us into satisfactory relations with objects to which the hypothesis points. The more true an idea is the more satisfactory it is. "At each and every concrete moment truth for each man is what that man 'troweth' at that moment with the maximum of satisfaction to himself; and similarly, abstract truth, truth verified by the long run, and abstract satisfactoriness, long run satisfactoriness, coincide." [103] Satisfaction is a constituent of truth, and the matter of the true becomes "absolutely identical with the matter of the satisfactory." [104]

Satisfactions reintroduce subjective aspects into the truth situation, this time at the verification end. James' philosophy now completes its circle. Consciousness has always been an organ functioning for the sake of personality needs and interests. Mental activity has been a means to satisfy these needs and interests via concrete practical adjustment to reality. Now success is the judge of the validity of that mental activity in providing for the satisfaction of those needs and interests. Needs and interests not only instigate the process but judge it as well. But it does not seem fair to leave James at this exact point, perhaps because the critics have stressed the needs of pragmatic naturalism as being essentially subjective and selfish. This is not exclusively what James meant, of course. Subjective satisfaction does play a part. If other things are equal, "these emotional satisfactions count for truth," but the other things must be equal, among them "being the intellectual satisfactions." [105] Some of these are love of consistency, of simplicity and unity. Each aids in nullifying an individual moment's selfish satisfaction. True satisfaction only occurs by considering all of these needs and interests, by recognizing previous satisfactions and, therefore, recognizing reality's (pure experience) own internal structure. Only in this way are today's hopes and beliefs built on the foundation of yesterday's achievements.

CHAPTER IV

PROCESS AND STRUCTURE IN THE METAPHYSICS OF JOHN DEWEY

William James felt that his pragmatic empirical method, based on *The Principles of Psychology,* did justice to all of nature. It took into consideration the connections within nature as well as the separations. John Dewey agreed with him. He believed that James' new psychology must be the glasses through which we should look in order to dissolve the fixed separations in past epistemological deadlocks. Everything is of nature and so we must consider everything as evidence in the attempt to disengage philosophical thought from these dead ends. Logical theory and the increasing perfection of experimental inquiry and the genetico-functional conceptions in science would serve as the instrument.

Dewey thought that the relation of thought to reality, and of thought to its consequences, lay at the very heart of the issue. He claimed that we assume the existence of thought as distinct from reality in the very way we present the problem, and therefore are already unfair to nature in its fullness. We think of both of these terms as absolute, fixed and predetermined. Therefore we think we can find a solution to the problem by understanding inherited premises which are already complete in existence. The separation of the ideal from the real is another, although related assumption, which lay at the heart of the epistemological problem. This assumption posits a realm more fundamental and more ultimate than that which we encounter in the changing world. Because of these *a priori* categories of mind we automatically understand the case as one of relationship, and this poses a problem: If reality already possesses the knowledge thought is trying to give it, thought is unnecessary: if reality does not possess it then thought is its own private business or even false and has nothing to do with reality.[1]

According to Dewey the solution is to take nature as it is and not try to fit our *a priori* constructions over its fulness. Of course, it is true that it is the business of thought to discriminate in a given situation of perplexity "between what is genuine and what is counterfeit, the veridical and the illusory, what is and what merely seems, what is valid or objective and what is invalid or 'subjective' "; but we must remember that these discriminations are ours, taking place in a limited setting, via a narrow thought process directed by a particular reason.[2] They are only "ends in relationships." As soon as we take these contextual discriminations as if they were absolutely given apart from a particular historic situation and context, we begin to force nature into our categories of thought. We begin to see it in terms of a metaphysical dualism that leads to epistemological deadlocks. We forget the instrumental practical character of our discrimination and treat it as independent and ultimate. We "hypostatize" discriminations that were at first instruments or functions in order to serve thought and then allow them to become a superior "reality" that transcends the thought process rather than arising within and because of it.

This hypostatization of local discriminations is the product of the natural tendency in man to crave the fixed and the sure. It represents James' "tender-minded" retreat into the certain, the traditional, the accepted. At times it may seem that this is the only tendency man does have within himself for he has devoted a great deal of his intellectual history to the satisfaction of it. The obvious example is the classical philosophers who devoted themselves to checking aspirations and desire. They assume that "measure, order, proportion, limit, is the nature of the world, and reason is the voluntary perception and intelligent adoption of measure as the rule of life. Instinct, fancy, aspiring desire, is the great enemy." [3] Automatically the subject matter of sense knowledge and opinion stand opposed to the subject matter of reason on ontological grounds, "that is, due to the very 'being' of the subjects involved." [4] Meanings of experienced things stand apart from the experienced things themselves and we can reach them not by turning to the experienced thing but by grasping its static unchanging rational form of genera and specie. This stands forever against the irrational, changing experienced thing.

The Middle Ages continued to think philosophically in these static terms, even long after actual knowledge in its most authentic form had adopted experimental methods. More surprising perhaps is the fact that later logical schools continued to use the static framework as that into which they had to fit their results of observation and experimental inquiry. Empiricism, for instance, takes "what is given in the thought situation for the sake of accomplishing the aim of thought as if it were given absolutely, or apart from a particular historic situation and context." [5] Rationalism holds "that ultimate principles of a universal character are the objects of immediate knowledge and that reason is the organ of their apprehension." [6] Each school created a form apart from the matter of everyday experience, a fixed static form outside of, and antecedent to, the experimental process of inquiry itself. Even the philosophies of flux succumb to the quest for certainty for in their denial of the sure and certain they "have deified change by making it universal, regular, sure." [7] Marx's idealization of the principle of conflict is still another expression of the search for the sure and the fixed.[8]

112

The whole hearted concentration on the fixed and the sure and its attendant ills is that from which Dewey wanted to disengage philosophical thought. His work may be thought of as an extensive attack on the fallacy of fixed ends and the fallacy of dualism. He attacked all "supernaturalists" who believe there are "considerations which do not flow from the course of experience as that is judged in terms of itself, but which have a significance independent of the course of experience as such." [9] Such tender-minded beliefs are dangerous not only because they render "men careless in their inspection of existing conditions," [10] but because this non-empirical fixed entity given prior to reflective inquiry is a deterrent to free inquiry. It is a consideration to which inquiry must finally agree. The static hypostatization becomes material given ready-made to the thought process and thereby is an authority held to exist in virtue of the inherent constitution of the universe. It becomes a law unto itself, a natural law, a final goal, a *summum bonum* which we must necessarily obey. Because goods, truth, ends, values are given in the sense of being completely there for recognition, all that we must do is to find them. "Custom, prejudice, class interests and tradition embodied institutions," become the determiner of necessity.[11] They become a shield for conservatism, "a standing still on the part of thought; a clinging to old ideas after those ideas have lost their use, and hence, like all superstitions, have become abstractions." [12]

In Dewey's own terms the disengagement called for is an attempt to rescue knowledge from epistemology and give it back to logic, which he defines as "an account of the ways in which valid inferences or conclusions from things to other things are made." [13] Man must conceive of knowing "as active and operative, after the analogy of experiment guided hypothesis, or of invention guided by the imagination of some possibility." [14] Thinking man must direct his attention toward the gross, macroscopic crude subject matters in experience and he must effect the development of "instrumentalities of inquiry, measurement, symbolization, calculation, and testing." [15] If there is to be a metaphysic it must grow out of this logical process and not vice versa. Thinking man must shift his interest from the wholesale essence back of special changes to the question of how special changes serve or defeat concrete purposes. He must shift from the idea of an intelligence which shaped things once for all to the idea of particular intelligences which are shaping things here and now, from the idea of an ultimate goal of good to the idea of direct increments of justice and happiness that intelligent administration of existent conditions may beget, and carelessness and stupidity may destroy or forego. Philosophy must take into account the sense of insecurity rife in the world today and forget the classical claim that the world in which we live is fundamentally one of fixed order, significance and worth. It should direct its attention to efforts to break down the apparent fixity and to induce change. The form that remains unchanged to sense, "the form of seed or tree, is regarded not as the key to knowledge of the thing, but as a wall, an obstruction to be broken down." [16] Science should be its example for it constantly moves away from acceptance of everlasting unchangeable elements and emphasizes interaction and the fact that interactions modify things. Man should understand differences between the apparently permanently permanent and the obviously changing as one of tempo or rate of change.

NATURE

Experience

Dewey's call is for a new method. He declares that we must reject inherent natures as such and accept empirical differences only as methodological. They are products of a context and their validity only extends into that context.

Just as science refuses to accept eternal conservative static things in themselves so philosophy must foreswear "inquiry after abolute origins and absolute finalities in order to explore specific values and the specific conditions that generate them." [17] Man must turn his concern to that which he experiences and from this alone gain his instruction.

It is interesting that both Dewey and James found it necessary first to assert a new method in order to do justice to the totality of nature. That new method in each case affirms the common sense world of everyday happenings as the foundation of thought. Our experience of it is determinate, and it alone is the adequate principle of control of objectivity of thought. In this regard Dewey also agrees with James' reference to Kant's empiricism and vindication of creativity, although I must admit he places a far more favorable aura around it. He says it was Kant who "put an end to the old attempt to reach conclusions about matters of existence, whether soul, external nature or God, by mathematical and conceptual reasoning. Concrete experiences, not logical conceptions by themselves warrant statements about matters of existence." [18]

As James did before him, Dewey saw that one of the first implications stemming from such an empirical approach to philosophy is that the experienced features of human sufferings, enjoyments, trials, failures and successes together with the institutions of art, science, technology, politics, and religion which mark them, are to offer a part of the reliable basis on which men build philosophy, simply because they are genuine features of the world in which we live. Expressing it rather succinctly, he said that we experience things that have quality in our everyday immediate contacts. Quality impregnates the unique, unduplicated character of an experienced thing. Hence, if we really wish to accept the world as the foundation of the thought process, we must take qualitative things into account as part of "reality." We must give everything we encounter in the world an equal hearing until experimental this-worldly methods prove them inferior. If we fail to do this we prevent nature from speaking for itself and submit it to an attitude in which some other realm or fabrication of ontological gulfs dominates. "Inquiry should follow the lead of its subject matter and not be subordinated to any end or motive having an external source." [19] Philosophy should follow the lead of modern day science in its movement away from fixed authoritative elements. For example, Einstein reversed the Newtonian policy of giving a particular discipline absolute authority to control theoretical development by giving the final authority to experimental findings. This led not only to a more honest and complete analysis of environment but to a realization that there is no ultimate fixed and independent substance in which mass, time and motion rests.[20]

Experience then takes into account everything with which it comes into contact. But it is necessary to say that we should not confuse Dewey's experience with James' pure experience. Rather, the latter is equivalent to Dewey's nature, and we could say the former is equivalent to James' stream of consciousness. Experience is simply "things interacting in certain ways." [21] It comes about by the interaction of man and nature, both being parts of nature, incidentally. It signifies active and alert commerce with the world, in fact complete interpenetration of the self and the world. "The self, the 'subject' of action—is a factor within experience and not something outside of it to which experiences are attached as the self's private property." [22]

Three important implications stem from this understanding of experience. The first is that all states and experiences are a product of this interaction. There are no states or acts which are not interactions. The experienced thing is a unity of object and subject, act and material. This is all there is, the one sphere of existence which includes the whole scheme of things. No experience can draw upon a particular and separate being for there isn't any.

116

The second implication is that man, because of his interrelation with the physical world, plays a considerable role in creating just what he is going to experience. This means experience is primarily an active process uniting man in his totality to nature. The relationship is "something dynamic and energetic. It fixes attention upon the way things bear upon one another, their clashes and unitings, the way they fulfill and frustrate, promote and retard, exist and inhibit one another." [23] There is now room for genuine emergence and change, adventure, choice and freedom as well as the uncertain and the vague. The alteration of prior existence is really possible. The human context transforms experienced things and events, both physical and social; while things previously external to the organism change and develop it through intercourse. The result is an open universe with plural and unfinished directions, with irregularities and hazards, with novelties and unadjusted cross currents. There is honest acceptance of the facts of science, a hopeful outlook for the future, and a courageous faith in man's ability to shape that future. Dewey unites philosophy with life.

The third implication is really an extension in two parts of the first two implications. Dewey defined experience as the interaction of man and his environment. The first implication stresses the fact that all states and experiences are a product of experience, the second stresses the role man himself plays in creating the state which he experiences. The third implication or extension concerns the experienced existent or the experienced object. It is at one moment a creation of the interaction of organism and environment and thereby a termination of the interaction, and at the very next moment nature absorbs it and it becomes part of the new environment awaiting interrelation so as to create or form still new objects of experience. The object of experience is what it is directly, yet as to its influence on later experiences it is transitional and possible. Each "that" which we experience is this combination, the termination of an interrelation, thereby form, and the beginning of a new relation, thereby matter. As to which context will dominate, form or matter, the static or the continuous, that depends upon the organism. Nature contains this mixture within itself awaiting exploitation and this very capability gives it its poignancy:

> If existence were either completely necessary or completely contingent there would be neither comedy nor tragedy in life, nor need of the will to live. The significance of morals and politics, of the arts both technical and fine, of religion and of science itself as inquiry and discovery, all have their source and meaning in the union of Nature of the settled and the unsettled, the stale and the hazardous. Apart from this union, there are no such things as "ends," either as consummation or as those ends-in-view we call purposes. There is only a block universe, either something ended and admitting of no change, or else a predestined march of events. There is no such thing as fulfillment where there is no risk of failure, and no defeat where there is no promise of possible achievement.[24]

The other part of this third "implication" is that the experience Dewey defines as the interrelation of organism and environment is nature's life. "The moments when the creature is both most alive and most composed and concentrated are those of fullest intercourse with the environment." [25] Without this interrelation there is only static completeness and predestination. Nature's poignancy or potentiality to be experienced is life, "for in the process of living both absorption in a present situation and a response that takes account of its effect upon the conditions of later experiences are equally necessary." [26] Nature is alive, a

118

pulsating flow from static response to absorption in a new situation, where one situation is both the response and the absorption, both the formed product of a previous situation and the matter for a new situation. The difference lies only in the function, a particular moment is to serve us as an end or as a beginning. Call the process what you will: structure and process, substance and accident, matter and energy, permanence and flux, one and many, continuity and discreteness, order and progress, law and liberty, uniformity and growth, tradition and innovation, rational will and impelling desires, proof and discovery, the actual and the possible, symmetry and rhythm, authority or contingency and freedom, final or material and instrumental, causal mechanism and temporal finality, pluralism and monism, intellectual and esthetic; these are simply names in order to capture a moment of nature and reveal its purpose. Giving them metaphysical or philosophical significance "is but a formulated recognition of an impasse in life; an impotence in interaction, [an] inability to make effective transition, a limitation of power to regulate and thereby to understand." [27]

The Experienced

Its Flow. In effect Dewey has made the same transition as did James and with the same instrument, experience. That is, he has made the transition from the realm of personal experience, or consciousness, to that of nature, or pure experience. This is also the transition from foreground to background or from method to metaphysics. He describes nature as a pulsating flow where static distinctions are moments captured by the organism for a purpose. What we experience as objects are the static distinctions made from a background of continuity beyond distinctions. Nature is a temporal reality within which there is an experiential continuum of content or subject matter, of operations of

119

inquiry and of biological and physical operations. It precedes man's distinctions so in this sense is neutral to them. "The stuff of the world is natural events in themselves neither physical nor mental." It is psycho-physical.

> Abandon completely the notion that nature ought to conform to a certain definition, and nature intrinsically is neither rational nor irrational. Apart from the use made of it in knowing, it exists in a dimension irrelevant to either attribution, just as rivers inherently are neither located near cities nor are opposed to such location. Nature is intelligible and understandable. There are operations by means of which it becomes an object of knowledge, and is turned to human purposes, just as rivers provide conditions which may be utilized to promote human activities and to satisfy human need.[28]

In nature the distinctions man experiences are really continuous with each other. There is continuity between lower and higher, physical and human, logical and biological, even between the organism and environment itself. For instance, "no activity (even one that is limited by routine habit) is confined to the channel which is most flagrantly involved in its execution. The whole organism is concerned in every act to some extent and in some fashion, internal organs as well as muscular, those of circulation, secretion, etc." [29] Within nature lie the principles of connection and organization. There is no gulf, no two spheres of existence, no "bifurcation." Rather, there is a continuity of flowing history, parts of which terminate when they become involved in the interaction that constitutes experience. These terminations are due to the human contribution, a contribution extended via the human being's active and receptive relations to the environment.

The fact that there is a background that awaits interaction, that awaits becoming an environment, means of course that there is a fringe beyond what we now experience. Prior to the interaction there is no organism nor any environment. There is only nature. The organism becomes an organism only when it interacts with a portion of nature and thereby effects experience. All experience is to this extent a product of a selection, a choosing of this environment rather than another. It is a taking from the given total field of nature. As such, experience is always in the context of that total field of nature as well as its particular environment and organism. Experience is still in the continuity of nature.

What all this means is this: Experienced objects are products of the interaction of environing conditions and an organism. They are the qualitative results of selective activity from the immediately given extensive totality of nature. Therefore they are secondary in origin. Objects are achievements, not gifts, and as such they are not absolute but relative to the use that we are to make of them. In other words, they are the functional or instrumental distinctions we make by activity within a total field. They are products of the conscious foreground reaching down into the total background. They are somebody's world, a product of somebody's juncture of organism and discriminated environment. They are material "taken out of the context of direct experience and placed in the context of material within discourse for the purpose of meeting the requirements of discourse." [30] We select the situation. We select the singular object of quality. Dewey calls the ignoring of this contextual selected aspect of the experienced world the philosophical fallacy: the conversion of a particular local situation into a norm and model. This fallacy is related to Perry's egocentric predicament which stems from ignoring the fact that the experienced world is only part of total nature. In the egocentric predicament "pure logic assumes that its forms of discourse necessarily constitute the total subject matter of logic." [31]

Its Structure. For the process of inquiry, the designation of the qualitative objects of perception as experiential sense objects or completions of an interaction is poor because these objects (or forms) have significance only in their relationship to the process about to begin. For the process of inquiry they are not objects, but subjects or data for further interpretation. They are not form but matter, not conclusions but hypotheses. This dual capacity is due to the basic facts mentioned above: that nature is living continuity and all experience has the double status, to be involved in the future and at the same time to be individualized and consummatory. The case is somewhat similar to finding a tool to be defective in a new situation when it was satisfactory in a previous situation. Earlier it was an object of perception, an end, now it becomes an instrument, a conception, an hypothesis, toward a better tool. The life movement is from vitality (nature), to equilibrium (object) and again to vitality (data). Each halt in the process is the object or finished article of the previous process and the data or material for the next process. The process is somewhat similar to that of mining; the movement from mineral rock in place, to pig iron, and finally to the manufactured article. The mineral rock is the object or the finished article of nature's process during the course of centuries, yet the miner sees it as the data for his process. As raw material it is similar to the original *res* of experience, flowing nature. The data we select from nature is equivalent to the pig iron for we extract each from a previous *res*, "for the sake of being wrought into a useful thing." Each is a completion of a process and the beginning of a new one. The final manufactured article is equivalent to the object of knowledge and marks the end of the process of mining and of a particular inquiry, yet marks the beginning of a new process, one which perhaps involves a consumer, the other new life situation.[32]

The key word in explaining the process is selection or discrimination. Each step is a further discrimination from the broadness of previous condition. Selection moves the process along from the first mass of quality to the qualitative objects of experience to the third stage of objects of knowledge. Thus, selection is an organic part of the process and not an arbitrary practical addition which we clap on after we complete the inquiry. We can say that it reaches down into nature. But the question naturally arises: Does nature give a free hand to selection? Is there not some way that nature reaches up into a particular experience? Why selection in this way or that? Is there not some criterion that transcends this particular process (within nature itself that presents itself) as a basis for selection?

The question is in effect: Is there not a criterion for selection that transcends the personal schemes in order to obtain personal ends? Dewey's answer is yes. The dominant problems and conceptions of the culture of the times as well as its own nature restrict the organism in achieving its personal ends. These restrictions express the fact that the process of inquiry is social as well as personal. It reflects and embodies the experiential continuum which both biological and cultural conditions establish. This asserts again that nothing exists apart from everything else. There is no such thing as an instantaneous inquiry and there is no such thing as a judgment (the conclusion of inquiry) which stands apart from what goes before and comes after. Inquiry is a progressive and cumulative re-organization of antecedent conditions and it must take into consideration the obvious facts of attention and interest on one side and the working of established and assured habits on the other. Selection is therefore restricted to only those possibilities which are actualizations of the natural fulfillments with which the process finds itself beginning and of those which are humanly relevant, fulfillments of human preferences. All thought processes commit themselves to satisfying these fundamental conditions. In effect, interests and conditions provide the direction as well as the restriction.

In the main, unconscious habit serves to express the effect of social groupings. On account of habits formed in intercourse with the world, we inhabit the world. Habit organizes our energies into certain channels, dispositions, or modes of response. Through habit we develop a special sensitivity or accessibility to certain classes of stimuli. Habit is a way or manner of action, not a particular act or deed. When we formulate a habit, it becomes, so far as it is accepted, a rule, or more generally, a principle or a law of action. As such, when one idea or act occurs, the series will flow without the intervention of consciousness or will. It thereby stereotypes action into a fairly constant series of acts having a common end in view. This is a necessary condition for intellectual efficiency, for without it there is only irritation and confused hesitation. It thus helps direct us in selecting from the continuity of nature in order to construct the objects of knowledge. It is not knowledge itself, however, just as the objects of experience are themselves not knowledge. It is rather the concretion of the past, or better, the controlling of the past, so that we can employ it for further work. It allows us to know.

In this way habits play the dual role of structure and process. They are the instruments by which we are to experience anew and eventually know, yet at the same time they are a product of previous experience.[33] They effect a reorganization of the past experience and at the same time act in their particular way because of that past experience. By means of habit, the creative vision that modifies the old past experience becomes the organ that perceives the new experience, yet it is always aware of the customs, cultural conditions and social groups of the old.[34]

Human preference which places a restriction on selection due to the nature of the organism itself is as real a limitation as that of habit. "There is no experience in which the human contribution is not a factor in determining what actually happens. The organism is a force, not a transparency." [35] The encompassing social medium sometimes stifles this human preference but, nevertheless, it is always striving to liberate itself and to make over social institutions into a more congenial medium for its operation. It does not exist in a generalized sense, but does exist in a related way in a particular organism with a particular temperament which is willing to fulfill itself. Just its presence serves its end: by directing attention, consciously or unconsciously, to that which is congenial to it. This is an important point because it makes clear that the workings and structure of the human organism (covered by Psychology and Morals when used in the broad sense) is indispensable to logical evaluation.[36] I mean by this that human needs and preferences are in continuity with logical evaluation and thereby effect it. Logical evaluation must, therefore, take these needs into consideration. "The conclusion is not that the emotional passionate phase of action can be or should be eliminated in behalf of bloodless reason. More 'passions' not fewer, is the answer." [37]

The very effort to take into account human preference is what distinguishes philosophy from the physical and biological sciences. The sciences "deal only with what might be experienced; with the content of experience, provided and assumed there be experience." [38] Philosophy, in continuity with psychology, tells us how this hypothetical experience becomes a "categorical unquestioned experiencedness" in some individualized life. "Science is compelled by its own problems and goals to state its subject matter in terms of magnitude and other mathematical relations which are nonqualitative." [39] Philosophy uses this verified and solid body but discovers the additional traits associated with use and enjoyment, those traits that consider the objects as an instrument rather than as an end. These qualitative traits are as important as the quantitative ones but in accepting them philosophy leaves the hypothetical realm of what "might be" for the realm of particular instances of what is. Therefore it is involved with the problems and needs of what is, and has the obligation "of contributing in however humble a way to methods that will assist us in discovering the causes of humanity's ills." [40]

Such things as immediate qualities, values and ends are intrinsically pertinent to that solution because genesis and constitution are related. Man is the creator of the dualism of quantity and quality as well as the dualisms of habit and thought, means and ends, practice and theory, feeling and thinking, willing and thinking, consciousness and action, intelligence and aspiration, practice and imagination, science and emotion, individual and universal, subjective and objective, freedom and order. When we recognize this, "when . . . biological functions are recognized to be indispensable constituents of inquiry, logic does not need to get enmeshed in the intricacies of different theories regarding the relations of mind and body. It suffices to accept the undeniable fact that they are necessary factors in inquiry, and then consider how they operate in its conduct." [41]

"Need" is the word that we may use to express these necessary factors in inquiry that are not included in science. It is an indication of what causes human preference. The latter only becomes a force if there is first a need, a trouble, a problem, a struggle, a discrepancy, a tension.[42] It is this condition that questions the seeming fixity of the organism's habit. The pulsating flow of life suffers an obstruction and it attempts to adjust to a new situation. In order to do so, the organism inaugurates the doubt-inquiry-judgment process. Before the tension arose there was no need of idea, of thought, but now the "implicit force of rationality," desiring to realize itself, struggles within the limitations of the problem to destroy the barrier and again return to the free flowing state. If the object, which is the product of degrees of selection within the thought process, were present in the environment it would secure this reunification of activity; so it becomes a desired or needed instrument to secure the preferred ends which the given problem estabblishes. Hence, the whole process of inquiry becomes contextual. Its value rests in solving the problem out of which it has risen, viz., that of securing a method of action to answer needs, transforming the disordered into the orderly, the mixed up into the distinguished or placed, the unclear and ambiguous into the defined and unequivocal, the disconnected into the systematized. It is the search for form, for orderliness, but it is a quest, a search, in the sense that we must make the goal, not find it. And in making the goal we must use the weapons at hand: intelligence, desire or impulse (ultimately need) and action. Intelligence is the clarifier and liberator, converting impulses into plans. Impulse is the forward urge of living creatures. Activity is the means to resolve the problematic situation. The process of inquiry or philosophy is that activity uniting impulse or desire and intelligence for the desired end.[43]

I have now discussed rather fully two restrictions Dewey placed on the selective process, that is, habit representing the effect of social groupings or, more generally, culture, and human preferences representing the effect of needs. We find a third restriction, that of natural relations, in that part of nature which is antecedent to the particular selective process. It represents the extent of nature's potentialities. Whereas the inquiring organism introduces the first two restrictions into the process, this natural restriction comes from the environment. It exists prior to the process of inquiry and suggests or generates the direction of that process. In this sense it is the subject matter for the final object of knowledge. The object as such doesn't exist prior to the process but this subject matter does. The matter for the self, needs, consciousness, etc., are all functionally selected relations from this nature which possesses them in a suggested way. They are products of nature's antecedent existence. In inquiry we never doubt this existence. Rather we "doubt some received piece of knowledge about some specific thing of that world, and then set to work as best we can, to rectify it." [44]

Dewey is actually making two assertions. The first is that there is a real antecedent to the thought process.[45] The second is that this antecedent presents obstructive and constructive conditions to the process of inquiry. It naturally bulges and naturally alters so to speak, and the job of knowledge is to seize upon these characteristics and develop them into objects of knowledge. To the extent nature has these natural tendencies, to this extent it has structure, or order, or organization. This is the stable element with the flow of nature, and as such is a necessary condition of all inquiry and of all knowledge.[46] It is that in nature which signifies a certain limitation of power toward a specific thing in a particular direction. It is that in nature which allows it to give birth to objects that stay with us as ideal. In general, nature must be such as to be capable of taking on our ideal logical form. Nature thus supplies material with the potential for the embodiment of our logical ideals. It lends itself to operations by which it reaches perfection and resists others that interfere. Different ideas have their different "feels," Dewey says, meaning thereby that the "feels" are signs of an intellectual stop and go, telling us when existence is capable of taking on the logical idea.[47]

"If experienced things are valid evidence, then nature in having qualities within itself has what in the literal sense must be called ends, terminals, arrests, enclosures." [48] If different "feels" are possible, then the material world of nature which furnishes exemplifications of them must possess characteristics that do exemplify them. What Dewey is saying is that the range of nature determines the possibilities of the range of inquiry. Thus logic finally involves itself in metaphysics, for its job is to map the field of activity and catalog the means and ends that it finds there. It deals on the surface with the process of inquiry, but since it must concern itself with objects of knowledge, it must ultimately reach thereby the structure of nature, the structure which allows nature to be so manipulated. Logic's concern is not only with recording the process of inquiry, but its concern is also with the metaphysical question: what sort of world has this ability to be so manipulated?

Yet we should never consider this structure of nature which allows certain manipulations as a structure existing apart from change or the process of becoming. Dewey believed that philosophy in the past had the tendency to conceive of a fixed state of affairs, the structure, as a latent or potential something or other that affects change. In reality structure refers to a characteristic of change, a concrete, actual, specific, existential change. There is not a structure plus change but only structured change. Structure is always in the context of the actual and overt features, which, interacting with other equally specific existences, bring about a particular change. There is, therefore, a priority or supremacy of method because the antecedent fixed structure is only so in regard to a particular process of change. For example, a house has a fixed structure but the structure is not something external to which the house has to submit. Rather, it is an arrangement of changing events, a constancy of events used for the particular consequences of building a house. We cannot lay down its structure in advance or define it except in context with this realized construction. It is a progressive derivation through differentiation under environing conditions.

Perhaps the word structure is too misleading. If so, the term relation can serve as a substitute. Certainly the term growth is more correct than fixed specie. There are natural relations with objective status, but it is an objectivity based on belief in the origin of species instead of the traditional belief of fixed natural kinds. The change is from the structural unit of composition to the controlling unity of function. This gives a new meaning to old constructions. "Faculties are definite directions of development; elements are starting points for new processes; bare facts are indices of change; static conditions are modes of accomplished adjustment." [49] The job is to transform the problematic situation into a resolved unified situation. In so doing it gains its metaphysical objectivity.

METHOD

Of course Dewey's interest is not with the structure of nature as an abstraction but rather with its effect on a practical situation. Remember, philosophy's concern is with what is. Therefore, the important thing to know about structure is that in context it always represents knowledge "imported from other situations." Its categories are really equivalent to attitudes, representing "a point of view, a schedule, a program a heading or caption, an orientation, a possible mode of prediction." [50] These categories are the result of the multitude of prior analyses, verifications and inferences occurring in a context. Structure is in effect the taking of the results of these limited experiences of nature and proclaiming it to be the meaning of the prior situation.

If this biased or partial view is going to have any "cash value," and this is the really important issue, we must introduce it to a new problematic situation in the further abstract form of a generic proposition. Its role in this raw process of inquiry is now meshed with that of habit and as such supplies the "rational" organization and system toward the satisfaction of the problem. Its validity as such lies in the recurrence of similar situations where these structural antecedent elements are built up. As an expression of this these propositions have a certain *prima facie* claim to recognition in new situations. But these standardized prepared views are not final. In reality they occupy a purely intermediate position, neither initial nor final. They are the bridges by which one experience passes over to the next. In this sense they are similar to every other static moment captured from the flow of nature. They are individual experiences or biases which we put into shape so that they will be available in regulating other experiences. They are generic propositions having inherent logical import because of their grounding in observational materials. As such they are normative laws, designations of relations sufficiently stable to allow the occurrence of forecasts of individualized situations.[51] But this structural law is only absolutely valid for the context from which we abstract it. Each context has its own qualitative emphasis, each selective inquiry operates in a unique biological and cultural situation. Each inter-action of environment and organism has its own structure, and that structure only exists in its functional relation to the process of inquiry in which it is directly involved. When we apply it outside of its functional base as a means of a particular production it has validity only as a hypothesis, a principle we tentatively employ as a method for conducting observations and experiments and for organizing special facts. It may well be that this application to a new situation will lead to a re-appraisal and a reformation of the principle. In this again, method and function subject the principle to re-appraisal.[52]

As did James before him, Dewey thus asserts that method has priority. It is to have supremacy over all antecedent situations in the effort to effect a union of theory and practice and of ideas and the operations they direct, in other words in the effort to know nature. He first places emphasis upon methods and only then upon the results obtained through reference to methods. It is this concentration of attention that Dewey calls for when he bids philosophy be more "scientific." It should pay more attention not to science's conclusions but to the method it employs. Scientific means "methods of control of formation of judgments." [53] He believed that its method is the method philosophy should follow because not only is it the most perfected way but, through the medium of inventions and technologies, it is the finally controlling and characteristic fact of modern life. This is philosophy's way of getting in touch with the practical reality of things. "If philosophy declines to observe and interpret the new and characteristic scene, it may achieve scholarship; it may erect a well equipped gymnasium wherein to engage in dialectical exercises; it may clothe itself in fine literary art. But it will not afford illumination or direction to our confused civilization." [54]

The paramount characteristic of scientific method that philosophy must absorb, if it is to make contact with nature, is the change from the qualitative or common sense measurement to quantitative or metric measurement, "from the heterogeneous to the homogeneous; from intrinsic forms to relations; from esthetic harmonies to mathematical formulae; from contemplative enjoyment to active manipulation and control; from rest to change; from eternal objects to temporal sequences." [55] The effect is similar to James' insistence on perception rather than conception. That is, Dewey suggests we discover the constant relations among changes rather than creating static definitions of immutable objects which are beyond the possibility of alteration. Science's method is to collect material that we qualitatively experience and then to select and modify it so that we experience certain relations. It disregards the qualitative heterogeneity of experienced objects so as to make them all members in one comprehensive homogeneous scheme, and in doing this it makes them capable of translation or

132

conversion one into another. Qualitative measurement is knowledge of isolated individuals occurring once and never again. Quantitative measurement is knowledge of "broad smooth highways by means of which we can travel from the thought of one part of nature to that of any other. In ideal, at least, we can travel from any meaning—or relation—found anywhere in nature to the meaning to be expected anywhere else." [56]

We might express the difference in views toward the sensible world. We may accept the so-called sensible world as objects of experience in which there are static ends complete in themselves in which the world consists of immediate beginnings and endings, not at all an affair of cases of knowledge but of the succession of qualitative dead events. Or we might accept the so called sensible world as data for knowledge, as a conceptual order, with flowing terms valuable for the future, a scheme of constant relationships by means of which we bind together spare scattered and casual events into a connected history. We experience both of these worlds, but as Dewey once said, the difference is whether we want to be "artists" who have their subject matter of experience, the qualities of things, or go on to be "intellectualists" or scientists, who have those qualities once removed.[57] The process is to get away from directly experienced qualitative characteristics but not away from observed material as such.

Again, I must stress Dewey's functional context. Just as the structure of nature is an instrument which we use in the form of a hypothesis, to solve new problems, so scientific method, the abstracting of qualities and the using of quantities, is a method which we employ to solve new problems. It is a process of selecting the homogeneous characteristics of objects through formulation in terms of relations of space, time and motion, so as to obtain the goal of unification of all facts and events. It unites the present situation with its accepted customs, beliefs, moral ideas, hopes, and aspirations with the past. It sees the historical process as a whole, as a union of experience and nature, of man and his world. It weds man and nature, possibility and actuality, personal response and objective material. It orders matter. But it does all this deliberately, that is, it does it as consciously undertaken activity for the purpose of obtaining desired relations and desired values.[58] Scientific method is an instrument in this sense. It is the forging and arranging of instrumentalities or tools for dealing with individual qualitative cases of experience so that the process of inquiry will eventually reach its goal; the object of knowledge, a solution to a problem.

In effect, this is Dewey's instrumentalist theory of logic. Via selectivity, it deliberately reorganizes qualitative experience into a clarified and systematized formulation of a particular process of thinking, and "projects method by which future thinking shall take advantage of the operations which lead to success and avoid those which result in failure." [59] These projections are the generic laws of philosophy, having logical or instrumental or metaphysical significance, if understood in a practical and experimental sense, but they do not have ontological significance.

EFFECT

So far this chapter has dealt with Dewey's process of inquiry as a functional mechanism and with the explanations of the foundations from which it begins to work. If attention stopped here, we could define the process as the scientific procedure of selecting quantities from qualities. But, as did James, Dewey directed his attention to the future. Therefore a more complete definition is that the thought process is the vital activity that brings into being new intended equilibriums of unity and coherence which we may immediately possess and enjoy.

This definition clearly brings out all three aspects of

134

the inquiring process: that of vital activity, of directed activity and of the verification of the activity. It is now apparent that action and knowledge are explicitly involved together. The process creates the object. Knowledge happens to things in the course of activity. There is no immediate knowledge. It stems from a problem and must solve that problem. It is particular and personal to that extent, for the problem is personal. To know something is to be responsible for it. In James' terminology, there is only "knowledge about," no "knowledge by acquaintance." Knowledge is literally something we do and finally obtain. The doing and the obtaining are so interrelated that knowledge just isn't knowledge until it is "done." That is, knowledge is not a matter of finding an existence which answers to the demands of the problem but is a matter of the systematic ordering of a complex set of data by means of the idea of the consequence as an instrumentality.

Here again, Dewey asserts the supremacy of method over the antecedent which we reconstruct. The things which we experience directly exist prior to being known but these things are not the same thing as the object of knowledge, the product of the reconstructive process.[60]

The difference in emphasis between the two definitions of the logical process of inquiry is not in the fact that the process involves overt doing, the making of definite changes in the environment, or in our relation to it. It lies in stressing the fact that anticipated consequences, which we construct in order to meet the conditions set by the needs of the problem inducing the active inquiry, direct this overt doing. The thought process takes place only when we intentionally perform operations and direct them toward anticipated consequences. It is the instrument which converts these anticipated consequences into knowledge. It is this concern with these consequences that distinguishes thinking from casual fancy and revery, for it is the anticipated consequence that controls thought by determining

135

the particular selections from the total field of nature. That is, thinking must "obtain that meaning or conceptual structure which is best adapted to instigate and direct just those operations of observation that will secure as their consequences just those existential facts that are needed to solve the problem in hand." [61] The consequences are the directives for the operation of experimentation, a sort of blueprint which directs and measures the process. They are functional and instrumental as well as descriptive. They are proposals for action as well as verifications of that action. As anticipations, they are hypotheses which help to direct operations which we will perform. As consequences they are the test of the anticipation. The anticipation, or a better term, the idea of the consequences, is a logical plan of action, an experienced possibility.[62] It is a draft drawn upon existing objects, an intention to act so as to arrange the objects in a certain way. It is a function so to speak, an arrest in the flux of events. If nature honors the draft or arrest, the meaning of the idea resides in a new experienced situation. It verifies the idea by its existence and solves the problem that started the inquiry. In this sense, the idea is a bridge from the brute factuality of the physical impression to the coherent value of thought's own content. Originally the situation carries the idea just as a mother carries a baby when the baby is part of her own organism, and then, due to social and biological needs stemming from the original situation, the idea effects a process of inquiry which culminates in the idea becoming an experienced actuality, just as a mother gives birth to a baby.[63] Ideas as such have their source in past experience, we find them in the objective situation in which we must solve the problem. This is all possible because man is continuous with nature. By thinking, nature achieves and exhibits its teleology; this achievement is not apart from it.

Now the actual process of inquiry begins to take final form. It is the procedure which passes from the crude subject matter to a highly specialized object of art. First there is the antecedent or condition that evokes thought. We partially experience it by the interaction of the individual and environment. In this form it is the qualitatively experienced object which concretely occurs and concretely effects us. It is still incomplete, and unfinished in its effect on us, and so must be converted into the data which is presented to thought. Finally it becomes the completed object of knowledge.

The idea is the weapon which accomplishes the third step of the process. Thinking always in terms of action, it recognizes the possibilities of development in the observed facts of data which are not now existing but which through appropriate action may be brought into existence.[64] This function of the idea invokes a preferential connection between present non-psychical data and the something absent, signified or meant by the non-psychical data. The present non-psychical data is the experienced qualitative objects of perception. They are the only evidence of the existence and nature of the objects which we infer, and they are the only checks and tests of that inference. These inferences are quite elastic, but as I mentioned above, the limitations of nature, biology and society do restrict them.

Hypothesis not knowledge is that which is absent, that which the non-psychical data signifies or means. It is short of being directly present. As the subject matter of inference it is a candidate or has a claim to become knowledge. It is a "surrogate" of some absent thing.[65] As such we may call it "thought" or "ideal," but only if we understand the terms in the functional sense of bringing about the transition from a relatively problematic experience to a relatively stable one. There is no ultimate "thought." Thought and ideal are a disposition of activity, a moving stream, a constant change, which has axis and direction, linkages, associations, initiations, hesitations and conclusions. It is constantly assimilating and reconstructing as well as directing toward the clear, the resolved, and the settled object of knowledge.[66] Only humans are aware of the ideal. All life interacts with its environment but only the human is conscious of itself, and can extend the here and now via the ideas which are potentially present.[67]

In order for the ideas to begin their inferential work, we must make them explicit, that is, formulate them into propositions of the if-then universal form. These propositions are products of provisional appraisals, evaluations of existences and of conceptions. They are means to the institution of final judgment which is the objective resolution of a problematic situation. Accordingly they are functional instruments in determining the objects of knowledge. Things and events are the material and objects of inquiry; propositions are the means of inquiry. They are the instruments which sum up the provisional conclusions of preparatory inquiries and record and retain them for subsequent use. In this sense, we can call these propositions causal, for they retain a content which is a relation of conditions that are means to other conditions that are consequences. This is their value. They formulate the rule and method of experimental observation, considering biological and cultural needs. They are regulative and formative in being functionally anterior to an experience. They determine the characteristic which must be found to exist in order to warrant the inference that a given singular is of a specified kind. They are necessary conditions of scientific method, but not sufficient conditions. They concern what is possible but their successes and failures must be constantly checked.[68]

Thus the existential basis of a universal proposition is directive action which discriminates and relates (orders) existential material so that it can in turn function as the ground for inferential conclusions. It serves as a limiting ideal or logical premise which states the intent of any proposition or predictive content. The element of relations which is a necessary prior assumption in order to accept its categories is not temporal and sequential but logical. Actions resolve qualitative occurrences into definite sets of relations. Thus, the law of generalization that expresses the conjunction of traits which these interactions determine contains no temporal relations, and *a fortiori*, no sequential relations. Experimental application tests its basis. Therefore it can never attain the status of inherent logical necessity, but remains a brute, particular fact. From the standpoint of nature, considering it independently of its subjection to inquiry, there is no criteria which determines whether we take some traits and omit or reject others. In nature everything is like and unlike everything else. The context is the thing.[69]

This discussion about universal propositions means quite basically that the idea, the logical instrument by which we abstract or select a limited range of conditions and relations out of the total complex of nature, does its work by using symbols (propositions) which designate possible operations, thereby making possible a great degree of exactness and intellectual organization. The idea provides the logical form, the postulate or the proposition by which abstraction or selection takes place, but the idea itself arises within the process which it is attempting to control. "While inquiry into inquiry is the *causa cognoscendi* of logical form, primary inquiry is itself *causa essendi* of the forms which inquiry into inquiry discloses." [70] Putting it more simply, Dewey says "forms regularly accrue to matter in virtue of the adaptation of materials and operations to one another in the service of specified ends." [71] Forms represent the propositions or premise; matter represents nature; and the specified end represents the idea. The proposition which imposes itself on to nature via selection fulfills in an ordered manner the idea for which we carry on inquiry. What becomes the end product is the subject-matter of logic, a reorganization of originally selected matter through the idea and at the same time a verification of that idea. It is an antecedent object in the sense that we intentionally arrange and redispose according to it, and it is an eventual object in the sense that we still must test or evaluate our arranging and redisposing by its presence. So long as the object remained in the merely "mental" status and was not an individually observed case of verification, it had the status of an inference whose content is hypothetical. As such it was a candidate or had a claim to knowledge which means that it still had to be tested. We can only derive the test from what is finally and immediately present.

It is with this insistence that the test of the process of inquiry be immediately present that the process comes to a close. However, there remains one point to develop, especially in the light of Professor Lovejoy's concern for asserting an ontological dualism. Dewey affirms that the final end product of the process, the object of knowledge, directs the process in the form of ideas, but he does not consider that end product completely constituted until the process is completed. The object of knowledge is in continuity with the process to the extent that its end and its beginning are related. Genesis is related to analysis, history to validity. In a time sequence this means there is no separation of past, present and future. Things of the past hung upon present observable events and future anticipated events which are capable of entering into direct presentation verify it. Past objects of knowledge cannot remain isolated in the past. In order to know them they must stand as "past-as-connected-with-present-or-future, or stating the matter in its order, of the present and the future as implicating a certain past." [72] The past-present-future events form an integral continuum so that we cannot take one part as complete and exhaustive "as such," without mutilating or falsifying the whole. The present supplies the data for a correct inference about the past and since the potentialities or meanings of the present depend upon

140

the conditions of the past with which it is correlated, we can imply future events as part of the present meaning.

Only when we connect the past event with a present and therefore a directly observable fact, is knowledge possible. We cannot know the event if it is an isolated self-sufficient affair. We need the past as required subject matter in order to make reasonable judgments about the future. Knowledge involves a connection and in time it is the connection of past, present and future. If the isolation persists there is no knowledge, for knowledge is the process itself. It includes its own means of verification. If we interrupt the process that point of interruption is data for knowledge, not knowledge. We might consider it knowledge of the past but we cannot, since the past is part of the process that includes its means of verification, the present and the future. Only in such a process do we know it and only by such a process do we know it. The object of knowledge is the accomplishment of the purpose of the process. The data we include in its formulation is included as the process tests and reconstructs it. The rational product grows out of the organic activity without being identical with that *from* which it emerges. For example, it is true to say that we do not make the bush, the star, the sun or the planet by inquiry, but that which we know as bush, star, sun or planet is a product of inquiry. The knowing process modifies the data of experience which will come to be the bush or star but it does not modify, so to speak, the bush or star after we know it as the bush or star.[73]

TRUTH

Earlier in this chapter I mentioned that we only know the object of knowledge if it satisfies the conditions which induce the inquiry. As such we can call it the consequence. Some people might call perceived objects such as oranges

141

and rocks objects of knowledge, but unless they are the culmination and satisfaction (the consequence) of a process of inquiry, they are arbitrary selections from it. To be known they must complete, fulfill, or lead out of a process. They must fulfill the functional purpose of controlling matter in order to solve a problem. Here the important point is that the consequence must have practical individual significance. "Knowing is, for philosophical theory, a case of specially directed activity instead of something isolated from practise." [74] Until we work the problems out in this practical immediate experienced solution, the idea which directs the process of inquiry is hypothetical. When the idea does satisfy the natural, the biological and cultural demands a situation presents, it becomes an object of knowledge, a consequence of the process. The whole thought process is dependent upon its aim, the aim is dependent upon the problem and the problem is dependent upon the situation in which it finds its incentive and excuse. The process is wholly natural because it originates in a specific problem and terminates in a specific test. The significance of the process resides in the test, in the consequence. This is what James meant when he said that general notions must "cash in." What this means in the whole picture of the process of inquiry is that the previous elimination of the qualities of experienced existence in the process is only an intermediate step. The elimination is necessary for the discovery of relations. In turn, these relations now become the means for controlled construction of new objects and institutions of new qualities. This new reconstructed consequence is a product of scientific procedure or art, it is a new concentration of quantity and quality. [75]

But note that Dewey ties the definition of knowledge to the consequence of a particular process of inquiry which an unsettled condition instigated. This instigation was the result of the interaction of a particular organism with a particular environment. Because of this particular character of knowledge, Dewey recognized the need for giving a different name to that generalizing process by which knowledge leaves its specific qualitative reconstructive situation. The name he chose for that process is intelligence, "the product and expression of cumulative funding of the meanings reached in these special cases." [76] It is the process which incorporates and funds knowledge or consequences into habits. And these habits in turn apply to new experiences. It is the beginning of a new process of inquiry and simply expresses again nature's essential character of life as I defined it above. It marks a shift of concern similar to that from object of perception to data for knowledge, from consequence to law, from universal proposition to generic proposition, from flux to structure, and, although not in complete agreement with Dewey's usage of the terms, from true to truth and good to value.

What guides us truly is true. The hypothesis or idea that works is the true one. Ideas, meanings, conceptions, notions, etc., are instrumental to an active reorganization of the given environment, to the removal of some specific trouble and perplexity. The test of their validity and value lies in accomplishing this specific work. If they succeed in their office, they are reliable, sound, valid, good, true. If they fail to clear up the perplexity, they are false. Just as it is necessary to tie down to specifics the first steps in the processes listed above, so we must tie the true to specifics. Situations only concern it in which we compare and contrast specific meanings and their already experienced fulfillments and non-fulfillments. When we experience the consequence, then we can say the original idea which called the consequence into being is true. The consequence itself is never true, rather it is the proposition which is true. Until we experience the consequence concretely, the universal proposition is hypothetical, neither true or false, just a mode of procedure in inquiry. At the moment of verification, however, the hypothesis becomes a captured moment of stability satisfying both the personal needs and the requirements of objective things previously captured, and it thereby becomes true. This is what James means when he says "truth happens to an idea. . . . True ideas are those that we can assimilate, validate, corroborate and verify." [77] Dewey expresses it as follows:

> . . . when there is a specific need for thinking, and a specific hypothesis emerges in response to the need, it is needful that we should have some way of testing its value, of developing it to the point of being true or false. And acting upon the hypothesis to select and collate data, to predict, to guide new observations and reflections, to organize the seemingly discrepant and to illuminate the hitherto obscure is the way. The success of the hypothesis upon and along this way is its truth.[78]

It is wrong, however, to think of this corroboration or success in material terms only. In fact, this attitude would be evidence that we have misunderstood the entire meaning of Dewey's philosophy. The needs and problems that instigate the process of inquiry are not necessarily material needs and problems and so the verification is not necessarily material. Words such as satisfaction, harmony, appreciation, and happiness, are equally descriptive of the effect of the true end product of thinking.[79] If we understand the term "good" as the satisfaction of the forces of human nature or the amelioration of existing ills, then it might more easily be applied to the corroboration than true, although the true is finally the good and the good is finally the true.[80]

The concrete way to true knowledge, then, is one that begins with conditions and acts of doubt, and proceeds through suspense, observation, suggestion, experimental manipulation, hypothesis-formulation and elaboration, and application of mathematical calculations. It finally ends with stability and harmony. However, this good and true idea must be capable of fruitful functional use in suggesting and regulating further inquiries so that it fully fulfills the chore in life's process that we mark out for it. In other words, it must remove itself from the particular consequent realm to that of law, from a particular true to the abstract noun, "truth." This is expressive of a looking to the future and seeing what can be done with the weapons inquiry has given. The procedure we must display is detachment, accumulation, and funding, the same steps necessary in the process from knowledge to intelligence. But just as Dewey understands all hypostatizations, truth is by definition subject to the outcome of the continued inquiries of the morrow and as such is provisional. As James would say, its validity lies *in rebus* and not *ante rem*. We hold it subject to use, and it is at the mercy of the discoveries which it makes possible. We must adjust it to the latter, and not the latter to it. Yet, in fact, it ideally represents the limit "toward which endless investigation would tend to bring scientific belief." [81]

Another term that serves this same purpose is value. Along with truth and intelligence, it heralds a new process of inquiry, whereas good, true and knowledge mark the end of a process of inquiry. When stress shifts from the good to what the good can do in the future, from the final particular consequence of the process of inquiry to how we can apply the static consequence to new situations and experiences, the terminological transfer is to "value." To call it value means that it "is never complete in itself, but always in behalf of determining what is to be done. . . . Judgments of value [as distinct from the direct experience of something as good] imply that value is not anything previously given, but is something to be given by future action itself conditioned upon [varying with] the judgment." [82] The result is the union of theory and practice, of thought and action. The conclusion of a previous process

145

of inquiry is the basis of values, but it receives final testing only by what we do in the living present, what we do in giving enriched meaning to other things and in increasing our control over them. It has claim on the process as does truth only in so far as the new process approves.[83]

Thus the complete naturalism of Dewey's philosophy ends and yet begins. He settles problems and needs, but the settlements by their very nature must activate themselves by encountering new needs. They are truths, intelligence and values in relation to the needs and problems of the past but they are only truths, intelligence and values if they determine the future. However, in the process of trying to determine the future they lose their static generic form and assume that of hypothesis. Thus, they not only begin in the flow of nature but they fall back into it, just as does everything else. Even the two fundamental assumptions that preceded the whole process of inquiry itself, the moral one that there is a sincere aim to realize true potentialities and the metaphysical one that nature possesses the common quality of amenability to the empirical method of science, have the same fate. They are born because of the need to find answers but their validity only stands with the future and as such they are hypotheses first, knowledge second, truths third, hypothesis fourth.

This movement from hypothesis to hypothesis sums up rather effectively the philosophies of James and Dewey. They see that each new practical and concrete situation demands a sweep on to a new hypothesis, but they also see that what is swept in the past and what is therefore installed as dynamically new becomes in time the matter to be swept away by new situations of the future. This is the way things are, this is the way nature is. It keeps the doors and windows open to genuinely new possibilities; it is incomplete, awaiting man's activities, awarenesses, needs and visions; it waits for our completions in order to gain value and truth; yet it always has at any given moment values and truths of the past.[84] Nature keeps its doors and windows open but only in a specified direction. This is the co-existence of process and structure. Nature says yes to the desires and actions of man but it also says yes to the inner grain of resistance that results in, and from, the flux only flowing in a certain way. Nature is neutral, prior to the comings and goings, but it contains them only in the specified way that they finally do come and go. Perhaps this is what Nicolas Cusanus meant when he asserted his principle of opposites. Nature says yes to the flux, and at the same time says yes to the flux as it practically flows in its specified way. It says yes to becoming but at the same time it says yes to being, that which limits the becoming to a specific way.

POSTSCRIPT

This book has given evidence to show that there is a congruence of basic themes or fundamental needs in philosophy and religion. It seems that these needs in turn stem from patterns of mental behavior that help to construct the philosophies or religions. To this extent philosophy and religion are art-products carved out of the experience which the pattern of mental behavior that does the experiencing determines. They are related to, and satisfy the demands of, that type of mental behavior. This is what W. H. Sheldon meant when he spoke of philosophy growing from "needs," and what John Herman Randall, Jr. meant when he called philosophy a "myth." This is what George Santayana meant when he said that "the great use of the gods is that they interpret the human heart to us, and help us, while we conceive them, to discover our own inmost ambition and, while we emulate them to pursue it." [1]

It is true that we could interpret this point in a subjective fashion; we could understand religion and philosophy to be *only* this expression of human needs and *only* human constructs to satisfy our desires and wants. The effect of such an emphasis is to deny to philosophy and religion a larger objective rendering of what is really significant in the world. This subjective interpretation would be similar to what the critics advanced when they considered pragmatic naturalism. Their implication was that process had little or no objectively valid place in the world.

148

But the recurrence in our studies of process as well as of structure indicates to me that the subjective interpretation is not complete. The recurrence of the theme of co-acceptance in both philosophy and religion substantiates this even more affirmatively. The fact that each religious culture studied finally found room for process and structure within its understanding of God, of what is ultimately significant in the world, and the fact that pragmatic naturalism, despite its bias toward process, found room for both process and structure in its understanding of Nature, of what is ultimately significant in the world, seems to indicate that both process and structure have a metaphysical or ontological status and with it objective validity.[2] This means that the needs of men do not exist first, and then create a philosophy or a religion in order to satisfy those needs, but that the larger being or reality which is true, or ultimately valuable, has within itself both the needs and that which satisfies the needs. As Nature has at once eyes and things that the eyes can see, so Nature, or God, has process and structure, needs and that which satisfies the needs. Ultimately both are in relation, and both are objective.[3]

Therefore it seems that in order to understand the full significance of the thesis that religion and philosophy are congruent to the extent that both interpret that which is significant in experience in terms of process and structure, and interpret the significant universe as embracing both principles, we must enter the realm of ontology. The question of being, of what is, is involved. Originally a philosopher's concern might only be with the method of correct thinking, as it was in the case of Dewey, and originally a theologian's concern might only be with a worthy response to the given reality, as it was in the case of, say, Ritschl; yet both concerns necessarily involve the nature of that which follows or demands that method or response. When we acknowledge this, we are in the realm of metaphysics. Metaphysics says reality must be of the sort that allows this particular method to be effective. The characteristics of the foreground must exhibit themselves in the background. Method "must in some way reflect or refract orders of things which are knowable orders." [4] Only by understanding our thesis in these terms, and accepting process as well as structure to be of metaphysical worth, do philosophy and religion take on a value that transcends the human whims of the moment.

A further step, I hope, can be made. It is one that concerns not the congruence of religion and philosophy but their incongruence. It is rooted in the findings of this book, but it also goes beyond the immediate evidence of it. If philosophy and religion are both necessarily involved in metaphysics to the extent that the first has at least an implicit understanding of what Nature is, and the second has at least an implicit understanding of what God is, and we can explain both understandings, at their root, in terms of process and structure, then it seems that, metaphysically speaking, Nature and God are, at root, the same. If this is so, the *difference* between philosophy and religion lies not in the fact that one is natural and the other is super-natural, but it seems from the evidence of the myths discussed in Chapter I and from the evidence of the discussion in Chapter II, III and IV that it lies in what is done with the common content, with man's relationship to that content. Philosophy, so it seems, is concerned with its interpretation of Nature, including man, or what it considers to be of ultimate value. Religion, on the other hand, seems to be concerned with the human response to what it considers to be of ultimate value. That is to say, Nature and God, the metaphysical and the "super-natural," philosophy and religion, seem to be the same, but the supernatural, or religion as expressed in particular historical religious manifestations, involves an addition of personal commitment. Re-

150

ligion is philosophy in its ontological core plus a superstructure of personal relatedness to that philosophy. Religion as historically exhibited expresses the something more of revelation, expressing the duties and rights which stem from the datum held in common with philosophy.

If this additional insight, and the previous metaphysical assertion, are valid, a particular manifestation of the religious spirit is not ultimately an attempt to answer the desire to believe or to belong. Nor is it an answer to fear or the desire for hope. It is rather an attempt to answer the questions of man's existence in terms of a basic definition of what is finally and ultimately significant. So understood, the history of religion is not just a comparative presentation of human organizations but rather a historical review of man's understanding of what is ultimately significant, of ontology, the nature of being, of God, *and* the meaning of our existence in relation to Him. In so far as we understand God and Nature as that whole of experience, including human needs, which is taken as absolutely significant, religion begins here and not with man. Religion and philosophy are both rooted, consciously or unconsciously, in an understanding of the universe. As man sees that universe, as man sees God or as man sees the ultimately significant, so he must act. It is true that man sees the ultimately significant through *a priori* patterns of mental behavior, but this only means man and the universe are in continuity; as Professor Woodbridge would say, the theory of knowledge and the theory of nature are simply differences in attention. In religious terms this means that God and man are in communication. Therefore the significant thing for the religious spirit is to understand God, and then on the basis of His nature as "seen" by the whole person, to act. Religion is the addition of personal commitment flowing from an understanding of the realm of the ultimately significant. Religion flows because of this understanding.

It is man's reaction to God. As God is, so man must act. The stress is not on what God can do for man, but what man must do in relation to Him. God is an end, not a means. Insofar as we direct attention toward this true end, we satisfy everything that is significant.

1. I have intentionally inserted the word human because to the extent that these attempts are meaningful to a human being they are subject to what that person "sees." The attempt to relate all experiences in the universe is subject to an *a priori* preference as to what the person considers is significant enough to relate and what he considers is insignificant enough to ignore. In other words, a previous understanding of what is significant in the world influences religious and philosophical attempts to relate various phases of experiences. Frederick J. E. Woodbridge expresses this point perfectly when he says that "we have come to learn that to call anything real exclusively, is to imply a preference, and that preference is largely a matter of the time in which it is born. It reflects an age, an occasion, a society, a moral, intellectual, or economic condition. It does not reflect an absolute position which knows no wavering." Frederick J. E. Woodbridge, *Nature and Mind* (New York: Columbia University Press, 1937), p. 100. This *a priori* "preference" is what I have tried to indicate by such phrases as patterns of mental behavior, types of personalities, or even James' types of mental make-up.

2. I am very much aware that orthodox Christian teaching stresses the point that the Father and Son each have characteristics representing both of the patterns of mental behavior. That is, in each symbol, both needs are expressed. Technically it makes this assertion by saying that the Father and Son are two, yet one, that they are diverse persons of one substance, or finally, that they are various hypostases of one

ousia. This means the Son does not express anything not already in the nature of the Father, and vice versa. Yet the fact of the existence of Son and Father means the Son and Father each symbolically do represent something special within that nature; otherwise there is no reason for the distinction within the godhead. My assertion is that the special quality Christianity asserts for the Son is redemptive action which implies relatedness to man. The special quality which it asserts for the Father is the judging action which implies transcendence from man. For quick and effective support I refer to C. C. Richardson's important book which asserts and develops the Christian implications of this polarity: His basic affirmation is that "the distinction of Father and Son is . . . a distinction about the paradoxical nature of God: absolutely above and beyond, and yet at the same time near and immanent. . . . The Father thus stands for God in his beyondness, the Son for God in his relatedness." *The Doctrine of the Trinity* (New York: Abingdon Press, 1958), pp. 21, 23.

NOTES FOR CHAPTER I

1. John Dewey, "Classicism as an Evangel," *Journal of Philosophy*, XVIII (November 24, 1921), 664-666.

2. William James, *Pragmatism* (New York: Longmans, Green, and Co., 1928), p. 22.

3. Morris R. Cohen, *Reason & Nature* (New York: Harcourt, Brace and Company, 1931), xii.

4. *Ibid.*, p. 9. See also Reinhold Niebuhr, *Nature and Destiny of Man* (New York: Charles Scribner's Sons, 1948), I, 10.

5. Charles Morris, *Paths of Life* (New York: Harper & Brothers, 1942), p. 77. In order to express this interesting polarity in religious, and especially Greek terms, it is not necessary to think exclusively of Apollo and Dionysus. Santayana wraps the dualism up in the one mythical figure Narcissus. He loves his form (thereby is structural or Apollonian)

but covets "that celestial object with an earthly passion" (thereby is enthusiastic or Dionysian). It is true that Santayana declares he is the "forerunner of Apollo, or Apollo in embryo, but in so far as he wildly pursues essence as if it were substance, he becomes Dionysus; . . . if on the contrary his intuition liberates the form of substance from its flux, and sees it in its wholeness and in its unsubstantiality, then Narcissus becomes Apollo." George Santayana, *The Real of Matter* (New York: Charles Scribner's Sons, 1930), pp. 30-31.

6. Charles Norris Cochrane, *Christianity and Classical Culture* (New York: Oxford University Press, 1944), p. 400.

7. It is approximately in the seventh century B.C. that the influence of Dionysus and Orpheus is felt on the Greek scene. Vittorio Macchioro, *From Orpheus to Paul* (New York: Henry Holt and Co., 1930), p. 213, and W. K. C. Guthrie, *The Greeks and Their Gods* (London: Methuen & Co., 1950), p. 115.

8. James B. Pritchard (ed.), "Ugaritic Myths, Epics and Legends," *Ancient Near Eastern Texts,* trans. H. L. Ginsberg (Princeton, New Jersey: Princeton University Press, 1950).

9. Marvin Pope, *El in the Ugaritic Texts* (Leiden: E. J. Brill, 1955).

10. Theodore H. Gaster, "The Religion of the Canaanites," *Forgotten Religions,* ed. Vergilius Ferm (New York: The Philosophical Library, 1950).

11. Pritchard, *Ancient Near Eastern Texts,* LL AB, 131.

12. *Ibid.,* KRT AI, 143.

13. *Ibid.,* II AB viii, 135.

14. *Ibid.,* I AB vi, 141.

15. *Ibid.,* AQ HT A vi, 151.

16. *Ibid.,* V AB E, 133.

17. *Ibid.,* III AB C, 129.

18. *Ibid.,* II AB iv-v, 133.

19. *Ibid.,* AQ HT A I, 150.

20. *Ibid.,* KRT A II, 143.

21. *Ibid.,* II AB, 132.

22. *Ibid.*, II AB ii, 132.

23. *Ibid.*, II AB v, 133.

24. *Ibid.*, AQ HT C iii, 154.

25. *Ibid.*, III AB A, 130.

26. *Ibid.*, I AB i and iii-iv, 140.

27. Theodore H. Gaster, *Thespis* (New York: Henry Schuman, 1950), p. 124.

28. Pritchard, *Ancient Near Eastern Texts,* I AB iv, 141.

29. *Ibid.*, II AB vii, 135.

30. *Ibid.*, II AB vii, 135.

31. *Ibid.*, AQ HT C i, 153.

32. *Ibid.*, I AB iii-iv, 140.

33. Gaster, *Thespis,* p. 129.

34. Theodore H. Gaster, "Ba'al is Risen," *Iraq,* VI (Autumn, 1939), 113.

35. Theodore H. Gaster, "The Religion of the Canaanites," *op. cit.,* p. 119.

36. "Baal," *Encyclopaedia Britannica,* 1955 ed., Vol. II.

37. I Kings 18:28.

38. Gaster, "The Religion of the Canaanites," *op. cit.,* p. 120. Baal's characteristics and associations express quite well, but in personal terms, the pragmatic naturalistic insistence, discussed in Chapters III and IV, upon the relatedness between the process of inquiry and its end product, the relatedness of organism and environment, and finally the insistence that the object known is in part a responsibility of the organism. El, on the other hand, is Dewey's "thing" upon which the "tender-minded" focuses his attention and because of which he makes limitation his principle of life.

39. Pritchard, *Ancient Near Eastern Texts,* AQ HT C iii, 154.

40. It was this very point, "protectors of the entire human race," that made the Eastern cults, which are traditionally immanent, so attractive to Rome, and gained for them so many proselytes. Franz Cumont, *The Oriental*

Religions in Roman Paganism (Chicago: The Open Court Publishing Company, 1911), p. 131.

41. Pritchard, *Ancient Near Eastern Texts*, I AB vi, 139.

42. *Ibid.*, III A B B, 130 and I AB vi, 139.

43. *Ibid.*, V AB D and V AB E, 137.

44. *Ibid.*, III AB C and III AB A, 129.

45. *Ibid.*, II AB vi, 133.

46. *Ibid.*, I AB vi, 139.

47. Gaster, "The Religion of the Canaanites," *op. cit.*, p. 120.

48. Arvil S. Kapelrud, *Baal in the Ras Shamra Texts* (Copenhagen: G. E. C. Gad, 1952), p. 87.

49. Elmer A. Leslie, *Old Testament Religion* (New York: The Abingdon Press, 1936), p. 161.

50. The "hero" demi-god, mortal strong man Heracles, who, after accomplishing his great work, "now lives forever with the immortals, where neither sorrow nor old age can touch him." Hesiod, *Hesiod's Theogony*, trans. Norman O. Brown (New York: The Liberal Arts Press, 1953), XII, 820-1022, 80. This is certainly an example, and by no means a single exception, of a confusion of the sharp clear lines separating the Greek gods and the people. It represents a breach of immanency in the transcendent picture of the gods as represented by the Olympians.

51. Plato, "Laws," *The Dialogues of Plato*, trans. B. Jowett (New York: Random House, 1937), II, Bk. VIII, 828. It is true, however, that Demeter is already one of the Olympians by Classical times.

52. Kurt Von Fritz, "Greek Prayers," *The Review of Religion* (November, 1945), p. 52.

53. Martin Nilsson, *Greek Piety* (London: Oxford Press, 1948), p. 52.

54. Herodotus, *History*, trans. A. D. Godley (New York: G. P. Putnam's Sons, 1921), Vol. III, Bk. VII, ch. 10, 319.

55. F. M. Cornford, *Greek Religious Thought* (London: J. M. Dent & Sons, Ltd., 1923), xix. In this sense it became

a punishment. Aeschylus tried to rationalize and moralize it. Sophocles expresses it in its full tragic significance, completely non-moral. See the discussion in E. R. Dodds, *The Greeks and the Irrational* (Los Angeles: The University of California Press, 1956).

56. Herodotus, *History*, Vol. III, Bk. VII, ch. 203, 519. "The gods could not tolerate human happiness beyond measure; therefore they debased the exalted from their high estate and humbled the mighty." A. LaMarchant, *Greek Religion to the Time of Hesiod* (Manchester: Sherratt & Hughes, 1923), p. 219.

57. Homer, *The Odyssey*, trans. E. V. Rieu (Baltimore, Md.: Penguin Books Inc., 1946), XI, 186.

58. Walter F. Otto, *The Homeric Gods*, trans. Moses Hadas (New York: Pantheon, 1954), p. 3.

59. Guthrie, *The Greeks and Their Gods*, p. 115.

60. Pindar, "Isthmian," V, 11, quoted in Cornford, *Greek Religious Thought*, p. 114.

61. Homer, *The Iliad*, trans. E. V. Rieu (Harmondsworth, Middlesex: Penguin Books Ltd., 1950), IX, 174.

62. *Ibid.*, XVI, 304. "Greek Prayer is merely the clear implication that there exists an inherent law of causation which brings to pass punishment for rash and criminal actions, and which, to some extent, may perhaps be modified by the gods, but over which the gods have no absolute power." Von Fritz, "Greek Prayers," *op. cit.*, p. 31.

63. Plato, "Laws," *op. cit.*, V, 741.

64. Homer, *The Odyssey*, VI, 107.

65. Hesiod, "Works and Days," 42, quoted in Cornford, *Greek Religious Thought*, p. 24.

66. Aeschylus, "The Eumenides," *The Complete Greek Drama*, eds. Whitney Oates and Eugene O'Neill, Jr. (New York: Random House, 1938), I, 307.

67. Homer, *The Iliad*, XXI, 392.

68. "Apollo," *Encyclopaedia Britannica*, 11th ed., Vol. I.

69. Otto, *The Homeric Gods,* pp. 78, 237.

70. Guthrie, *The Greeks and Their Gods,* p. 73.

71. "Apollo," *Encyclopaedia Britannica.*

72. Guthrie, *The Greeks and Their Gods,* pp. 183, 184.

73. Plato, "Charmides," *The Dialogues of Plato,* trans. B. Jowett (New York: Random House, 1937), I, 64.

74. Homer, *The Iliad,* I, 39; Hesiod's *Theogony,* I, 1-115, 55.

75. Otto, *The Homeric Gods,* pp. 76, 77. I don't think the picture is quite as neat as this, however. Apollo was also considered as the god of the healing art as Otto himself acknowledges, even at times considered to be the father of Asclepios. This attribute doesn't fit in any too well with distance. It definitely clouds the sharpness of Apollo's picture as painted by Otto.

76. Plato, "Republic," *The Dialogues of Plato,* trans. B. Jowett (New York: Random House, 1937), I, Bk. IV, 427.

77. Herodotus, *History,* II, Bk. IV, Ch. 161, 365.

78. Homer, *The Odyssey,* Bk. VIII, 124, and *The Iliad,* Bk. IX, 171.

79. This compromising of the clear character of Apollo should not be a complete surprise, nor should the compromising of Dionysus. If a society uses a god for a long time and if he plays an important role in that society, it is altogether likely that he will eventually reflect the full needs of that society.

80. Apollodorus, *The Library,* trans. James George Frazer (London: William Heinemann, 1921), I, Bk. IV, Ch. I, 27.

81. Cohen, *Reason & Nature,* p. 51.

82. Friedrich Nietzsche, "Ecce Homo," *The Philosophy of Nietzsche* (New York: The Modern Library, 1927), p. 868.

83. Apollodorus, *The Library,* I, Bk. III, Ch. 2.

84. Clement of Alexandria, "Exhortation to the Greeks," Ch. II, 15, quoted in Cornford, *Greek Religious Thought,*

p. 57. Pausanias says: "The first to introduce Titans into poetry was Homer, representing them as gods down in what is called Tartarus. . . . From Homer the name of the Titans was taken by Onomacritus, who in the orgies he composed for Dionysus made the Titans the authors of the god's sufferings." Pausanias, *Description of Greece,* trans. W. H. S. Jones (London: William Heinemann, 1918), IV, Bk. VIII, Ch. 37, 87.

85. Olympiodoros on Plato's "Phaedo," 61C, quoted in Frederick C. Grant, *Hellenistic Religions* (New York: The Liberal Arts Press, 1953), p. 108. The logical religious implication of this doctrine is some sort of immortality. "Happy is he among deathly man who hath beheld these things [the mysteries of Demeter] and he that is uninitiable, and hath no lot in them, hath never equal lot in death beneath the murky gloom." Homer, "Hymn to Demeter," *Homeric Hymns,* trans. Andrew Lang (New York: Longmans, Green & Co., 1899), p. 210. This seed of implication is what Orpheus later exploited.

86. Euripides, "Bacchae," *The Complete Greek Drama,* trans. Gilbert Murray (New York: Random House, 1938), II, 216, p. 234.

87. Edwin Rohde, *Psyche,* trans. W. B. Hillis (London: Kegan Paul, Trench, Trubner & Co., Ltd., 1925), p. 245.

88. Homer, *The Iliad,* Bk. XIV, 265.

89. *Ibid.,* Bk. VI, 120. In *The Odyssey* two references are made: Homer, *The Odyssey,* Bk. XXIV, 353, and Bk. XI, 180. Neither casts any further light on the nature of Dionysus.

90. Rohde says that "the Homeric poems do not recognize Dionysus as belonging to the gods of Olympus but they are aware of his existence." Rohde, *Psyche,* p. 256. From the Homeric poems themselves, I wonder if this can be legitimately asserted.

91. Cornford, *Greek Religious Thought,* p. 52; Rohde,

Psyche, 158; Guthrie, *The Greeks and Their Gods,* p. 34. In this regard it is interesting to note the recent findings of the name Dionysos in tablets in Minoan linear B script at Pylos.

92. Euripides, "Bacchae," *op. cit.,* 271, p. 236.

93. Plutarch, "Of Isis and Osiris," *Morals,* trans. William Baxter (Boston: Little Brown & Co., 1871), IV, Ch. 34, 95.

94. Homer, "Hymn to Dionysus," *Homeric Hymns,* trans. Andrew Lang (New York: Longmans, Green & Co., 1899), p. 239.

95. Euripides, "Bacchae," *op. cit.,* p. 227.

96. *Ibid.,* 772, p. 255; 275, p. 236.

97. Von Fritz, "Greek Prayers," *op. cit.,* p. 24.

98. Homer, "Hymn to Demeter," *op. cit.,* p. 183. As Dionysus was sometimes identified with Osiris, she (Demeter) has been identified with Isis. Plutarch, "Of Isis and Osiris," *op. cit.,* Ch. 34, 95, and Cumont, *The Oriental Religions in Roman Paganism,* p. 76. The Greeks considered her as the embodiment of the fruitful earth, giver of life and fertility to plants, animals and men. When she was in grief over the rape of her daughter by the lord of the underworld, Pluto, she neglected her occupation and there was a cessation of the fruits of the earth. Guthrie, *The Greeks and Their God,* p. 283.

99. This is the same principle that explains the development of astrology and magic. As the Stoics explained it, the world is considered as a vast organism, all the parts of which are connected through an unceasing exchange of molecules of effluvia. The stars as inexhaustible generators of energy are acting constantly upon the earth and upon man. Man himself is the epitome of all nature, a "microcosm" whose every element corresponds to some part of the starry sky. Magic based its interests not on the relationship between the stars in the heavens and the material world but on the

relationship of things of this world and assumed they effected each other. See Cumont, *The Oriental Religions in Roman Paganism,* pp. 171, 183.

100. Aristophanes, "The Frogs," *The Complete Greek Drama,* trans. Gilbert Murray (New York: Random House, 1938), II, 360, p. 941.

101. Guthrie, *The Greeks and Their Gods,* pp. 160, 179; Jane E. Harrison, *Prolegomena to the Study of Greek Religion* (Cambridge: University Press, 1908), p. 363.

102. Rohde, *Psyche,* p. 261.

103. Rohde, *Psyche,* p. 288. Carter, for instance, tells us that the Oracles inspired by Apollo on their first recorded use in Rome, in 496 B.C., introduced Demeter, Kore and Dionysus. Jesse B. Carter, *The Religion of Numa* (New York: Macmillan Co., 1906), p. 72. Perhaps the confusion centering about Orpheus' allegiance could be another historical example. Compare, for instance, Herodotus, *History,* I, Bk. II, Ch. 81, 367, with Pindar, "Pythian Odes," *The Odes of Pindar,* trans. John Sandys (London: William Heinemann, 1915), Ode IV, 176, p. 217.

104. Plutarch, "Of E at Apollo's Temple in Delphi," *Morals,* trans. William Baxter (Boston: Little Brown & Co., 1871), IV, Ch. 9, 486.

105. *Ibid.* Ch. 9, 488. I wonder if this didn't have fertility significance. Is not the invocation of Dionysus during the three winter months similar to the invocation of Baal during the time he was under Mot's power?

106. *Ibid.,* Ch. 9, 487.

107. Pausanias, *Descriptions of Greece,* II, Bk. III, Ch. 19, 119.

108. Plutarch, "Of E at Apollo's Temple in Delphi," *op. cit.,* Ch. 9, 487.

109. Morris, too, generalizes from his Greek base. For instance, Vishnu, Confucianism, Aquinas' Christianity (therefore Aristotle), and the Enlightenment are all labeled

Apollonian more or less, while Siva, Surrealism, Blake, and Euripides are in one place or another marked off as Dionysian. But he doesn't use these "representations" to substantiate his paths. They are just interesting generalizations. Morris, *Paths of Life,* pp. 124, 119, 195, 196, 160.

110. While the Cappadocians tend to think of the distinction between Father and Son in these terms, it is by no means clearly established that in fact this is the traditional Christian distinction. For instance, the Son is known as the Logos, and this certainly gives Him some right to be considered as the structural principle. The root of this difficulty stems from the Christian insistence that the *complete* identical Godhead is in *each* hypostasis. This is the doctrine of co-inherence or *perichoresis.* See also note 2 in introduction.

111. The fact that the final definition of the nature of the Godhead is in terms of three hypostases rather than in terms of two seems to me to be akin to Morris' introduction of Prometheus into his Greek mythical types. Each may be a necessary addition to set things straight but each symbolically does represent an addition to the two types of mental make-up. The Creed of Nicea, and I do not mean the "Nicene Creed" of 381 A.D., hardly gave thought to the place of the Holy Spirit and earlier records are not much more explicit. The New Testament is obscure and early writers tended to confuse the Son with the Holy Spirit. See, for example, "The Shepherd of Hermas," *The Apostolic Fathers,* ed. Ludwig Schopp, et al. ("The Fathers of the Church," New York: Cima Publishing Co., 1946), parable 5, Ch. 6, Section 5; and "II Clement," Chps. 9, 5. Nietzsche considers the inner core of the Prometheus myth ("the necessity for crime imposed on the titanically striving individual") to be un-Apollonian. It therefore represents an addition too. Nietzsche, "The Birth of Tragedy," *op. cit.,* p. 999.

112. Basil, "Letter 236," *A Select Library of Nicene and*

Post Nicene Fathers, ed. Philip Schaff, et al. (Second Series; New York: The Christian Literature Company, 1895), VIII, Ch. 6.

113. The tendency, springing from Cappadocian Platonism, is to consider the *ousia* as a philosophical unit, disclosed by internal analysis, and to consider the *hypostasis* as an external concrete independence. The saving grace is the Aristotelian distinction and the Aristotelian unity of the possible meanings of *ousia*. *Ousia,* essence, can mean that which is common to individuals or that existence of an individual. In Platonism with its existence of an ideal world apart from the phenomenal, the tendency was to abstract *ousia,* separating that which is common to individuals from particular individuals. Aristotle denied the existence of the ideal world apart from the phenomenal and so asserted the concrete *ousia,* that which is common to individuals exists in the individuals' species. *Ousia* in this second true Aristotelian sense is what orthodox thought accepted. This can be seen by their usage of "modes of being" or "three spheres of conscious being," which denote a transcending concrete unity. See for example Gregory of Nyssa, "On Not Three Gods," *Christology of the Later Fathers,* ed. Edward R. Hardy ("The Library of Christian Classics"; Philadelphia: Westminster Press, 1944). This second sense of understanding *ousia,* the Aristotelian, destroys tritheism because *ousia* is a single, metaphysical, objective reality. God regarded from the point of view of internal analysis is one object. God regarded from the point of view of external presentation is three objects. The Father, Son, Holy Spirit, are the Godhead. They are the same *ousia.*

114. It "is an impiety to say that God subsists, and is a subject in relation to His own goodness, and that this goodness is not a substance or rather essence, and that God Himself is not His own goodness, but that it is in Him as in a subject, and hence it is clear that God is improperly called: substance, in order that He may be understood to be

164

by the more usual name essence, which he is truly and properly called: so that perhaps it is right that God alone should be called essence." Augustine, "De Trinitate," *A Select Library of the Nicene and Post Nicene Fathers,* ed. Philip Schaff, et. al. (First Series; Buffalo: Christian Literature Company, 1887), III, 7,5,10 and 5,9,10.

115. *Ibid.,* 15,14,23.

Notes for Chapter II

1. Structure and transcendence are related in that each turns its attention to that which measures life and therefore stands apart from that which it measures, whereas process and immanency are related in that each turns its attention to the life process itself. For the former, that which controls man is of significance while for the latter, man himself is of significance.

2. From time to time in this chapter I have identified the critics of pragmatic naturalism as Our Critics in order to establish an over-all label of reference. I believe the mass of critics can be so related as I hope the rest of this chapter will substantiate. I do not, however, claim that the critics have a relatedness beyond what I have brought out in the chapter. They *are* related in their criticism of pragmatic naturalism as a philosophy because it generally sacrifices structure and they *are* related in asserting that structure must therefore be given a more substantial place in the total understanding of the universe. They *are not* related in their positive contribution as to just how this structure is expressed in the universe and they *are not* related in their understanding of the positive place process has in the ultimately significant aspect of the universe. Some are far more sympathetic to the value of process than others. In so far as these sympathies and these positive contributions contribute to an understanding of their criticisms of pragmatic naturalism, they have been developed, but essentially this

chapter deals with Our Critics only as critics, and not as positive philosophers in their own right.

3. William James, *Essays in Radical Empiricism,* ed. Ralph Barton Perry (New York: Longmans Green and Co., 1912), p. 160.

4. James, *Pragmatism,* p. 49.

5. Dewey sums all this up when he comments on Montague's *The Ways of Knowing:* "I have never taught that all needs are practical, but simply that no need could be satisfied without action. Our needs originate out of needs that at first were practical, but the development of intelligence transforms them so that they are now aesthetic, scientific, and moral needs. I have never said that thought exists for the sake of action. On the contrary, it exists for the sake of specific consequences, immediate values, etc. What I have insisted on is quite a different point, namely, that action is involved in thinking and existential knowing, is part of the function of reaching immediate non-practical consequences." William Pepperill Montague, *The Ways of Knowing* (London: George Allen & Unwin Ltd., 1925), p. 135.

6. Edward Gleason Spaulding, "A Reply to Professor Dewey's Rejoinder," *Journal of Philosophy,* VIII (October 12, 1911), 572.

7. Frederick J. E. Woodbridge, "Experience & Dialectic," *Journal of Philosophy,* XXVII (May 8, 1930), 268.

8. A. W. Moore, "Some Lingering Misconceptions of Instrumentalism," *Journal of Philosophy,* XVII (September 9, 1920), 518.

9. Harold Chapman Brown, "Review of Dewey's Essays in Experimental Logic," *Journal of Philosophy,* XIV (April 26, 1917), 246.

10. Josiah Royce, "The External and the Practical," *The Philosophical Review,* XIII (March, 1904), 118.

11. Wendell T. Bush, "Constructive Intelligence," *Journal of Philosophy,* XIV, (September 13, 1917), 519.

12. C. I. Lewis, "Review of Dewey's the Quest for Certainty," *Journal of Philosophy*, XXVII (January 2, 1930), 21.

13. George Santayana, *Winds of Doctrine* (London: J. M. Dent & Sons, Ltd., 1913), 208.

14. John Herman Randall, Jr., "Instrumentalism & Mythology," *Journal of Philosophy*, XVI (June 5, 1919), 316; George Santayana, "Dewey's Naturalistic Metaphysics," *Journal of Philosophy*, XXII (December 3, 1925), 680.

15. Cohen, *Reason & Nature*, p. 450. Cohen also adds: "Why should the word life itself be a term of praise except to those who prefer the primitive and dislike intellectual effort?" *Ibid.*

16. Ralph Barton Perry, "A Review of Pragmatism as a Theory of Knowledge," *Journal of Philosophy*, IV (July 4, 1907), 372.

17. Santayana, *Winds of Doctrine*, p. 207.

18. John Russell, "Some Difficulties with the Epistemology of Pragmatism and Radical Empiricism," *The Philosophical Review*, XV (July, 1906), 406.

19. W. H. Sheldon, "The Vice of Modern Philosophy," *Journal of Philosophy*, XII (January 7, 1915), 6, 10, 12.

20. Randall, "Instrumentalism & Mythology," *op. cit.*, 309-311.

21. W. P. Montague, "The New Realism and the Old," *Journal of Philosophy*, IX (January 18, 1912), 39.

22. A. W. Moore, "Some Lingering Misconceptions of Instrumentalism," *op. cit.*, p. 518.

23. Niebuhr, *Nature and Destiny of Man*, I, 75.

24. R. W. Sellars, "Professor Dewey's View of Agreement," *Journal of Philosophy*, IV (August 1, 1907), 434.

25. Cohen, *Reason & Nature*, p. 426.

26. *Ibid.*, p. 368.

27. *Ibid.*, pp. 225, 446, 456.

28. *Ibid.*, p. 19. See also pp. 106, 157, 162, 203, 412, 365.

29. *Ibid.*, p. 68.

30. Frederick J. E. Woodbridge, "Behavior," *Journal of Philosophy*, XXII (July 16, 1925), 405.

31. Frederick J. E. Woodbridge, *An Essay on Nature* (New York: Columbia University Press, 1940), p. 192.

32. *Ibid.*, pp. 56, 191; Woodbridge, "Behavior," *op. cit.*, pp. 402, 404.

33. Arthur O. Lovejoy, "Pragmatism as Interactionism," *Journal of Philosophy*, XVII (October 21, 1920; November 4, 1920), 629.

34. William Ernest Hocking, "Action and Certainty," *Journal of Philosophy, XXVII* (April 24, 1930), 232.

35. Royce, "Eternal and Practical," *op. cit.*, p. 137. See also Murphy's and Russell's articles in *The Philosophy of John Dewey*, ed. Paul Arthur Schilpp (New York: Tudor Publishing Company, 1939). All ignore to some extent that fact of reference to problematic situation.

36. W. H. Sheldon, "Review of Studies in Logical Theory," *Journal of Philosophy*, I (February 18, 1904), 103.

37. B. H. Bode, "Cognitive Experience and Its Object," *Journal of Philosophy*, II (November 23, 1905), 661.

38. Arthur O. Lovejoy, "The Thirteen Pragmatisms," *Journal of Philosophy*, V (January 2, 16, 1908), 35. See also Santayana, "Dewey's Naturalistic Metaphysics," *op cit.*, p. 677.

39. W. P. Montague, "Studies in the History of Ideas," quoted in J. R. Kantor, "Instrumental Transformism and the Un-Realities of Realism," *Journal of Philosophy*, XVI (August 14, 1919), 452. See also Daniel Sommer Robinson, "An Alleged New Discovery in Logic," *Journal of Philosophy*, XIV (April 26, 1917), 231; B. H. Bode, "Intelligence and Behavior," *Journal of Philosophy*, XVIII (January 6, 1921), 14; Niebuhr, *Nature and the Destiny of Man*, I, 27; Perry, "A Review of Pragmatism as a Theory of Knowledge,"

168

op. cit., p. 373; Bush, "Constructive Intelligence," *op. cit.,* p. 508.

40. George Santayana, "Two Rational Moralists," *Journal of Philosophy,* XIII (May 25, 1916), 290.

41. John Dewey, "Experience, Knowledge and Value: A Rejoinder," *The Philosophy of John Dewey,* ed. Paul Arthur Schilpp (New York: Tudor Publishing Company, 1939), p. 565.

42. Cohen, *Reason & Nature,* p. 80.

43. *Ibid.,* p. 75.

44. W. P. Montague, "May a Realist Be a Pragmatist: Implications of Instrumentalism," *Journal of Philosophy,* VI (September 2, 1909), 487.

45. Evander Bradley McGilvary, "Pure Experience and Reality," *The Philosophical Review,* XVI (May, 1907), 276. For an interesting discussion that contains both criticisms within one space see B. H. Bode, "The Concept of Pure Experience," *The Philosophical Review,* XIV (November, 1905).

46. Woodbridge, *An Essay on Nature,* p. 284.

47. *Ibid.,* p. 195.

48. John Grier Hibben, "The Test of Pragmatism." *The Philosophical Review,* XVII (July 1908), 381. See also Woodbridge, "Behavior," *op. cit.,* 405; Woodbridge, *An Essay on Nature,* p. 273; Lovejoy, "The Thirteen Pragmatisms," *op. cit.,* 36; and Lovejoy, "Pragmatism as Interactionism," *op. cit.,* 630. Reason is always the source of this structure for "the conceptual in knowledge is the element of pure structure or operational construction. C. I. Lewis, "Pragmatism and Current Thought," *Journal of Philosophy,* XXVII (April 24, 1930), 243; Niebuhr, *Nature and Destiny of Man,* II, 14. In a sense, the cry is not for life but the good life. The implication is that pragmatic naturalism cannot define the good, only rationalism. Cohen, *Reason & Nature,* p. 457.

49. Santayana, *Winds of Doctrine,* p. 209.

50. Frederick J. E. Woodbridge, "The Promise of Pragmatism," *Journal of Philosophy,* XXVI (September 26, 1929), 543.

51. Santayana, "Dewey's Naturalistic Metaphysics," *op. cit.,* p. 675.

52. Hocking, "Action and Certainty," *op. cit.,* p. 228.

53. Santayana, "Dewey's Naturalistic Metaphysics," *op. cit.,* p. 674. Chapter four explores the validity of these assumptions.

54. Niebuhr, *Nature and Destiny of Man,* I, 124.

55. Sheldon, "Review of Studies in Logical Theory," *op. cit.,* p. 105.

56. *Ibid.,* p. 103.

57. Woodbridge, "Behavior," *op. cit.,* p. 409.

58. Cohen, *Reason and Nature,* p. 83.

59. *Ibid.,* p. 45.

60. *Ibid.,* p. 135. Woodbridge says "the only magic worth having is that born of a happy marriage of sense and intellect." *An Essay on Nature,* p. 242. This essentially is the same assertion as made by Cohen but it saves one of the poles from the label of irrational. Cohen has no hesitancy with using the word and, in fact, in accord with Lovejoy, marks off pragmatic naturalism as he understands it, as a critic, as anti-rationalism. *Ibid.,* p. 157; Arthur O. Lovejoy, "Present Philosophical Tendencies," *Journal of Philosophy,* IX (November 7, 1912), 631.

61. Morris R. Cohen, "The Distinction between the Mental and the Physical," *Journal of Philosophy,* XIV (May 10, 1917), 262.

62. Cohen, *Reason & Nature,* xiii.

63. *Ibid.,* p. 69.

64. *Ibid.,* p. 114. The kinship that this criticism has with the basic categories of pragmatic naturalism is evident when the structure demanded is explained in terms of relations. Woodbridge is completely in harmony with this interpreta-

tion as seen above. His definition of mathematics as "variables which in spite of varying keep a balance and are in that sense in the grip of fate" is further evidence. Woodbridge, *An Essay on Nature,* p. 238.

65. "Reference to such possible application is essential to their meaning." Cohen, *Reason & Nature,* p. 126.

66. *Ibid.,* p. 230.

67. *Ibid.,* p. 157.

68. Independency yes, but only to the relative extent discussed above. Always there is the fundamental assumption that the logically necessary relations which hold between mathematical expressions hold of natural phenomena too. *Ibid.,* p. 225.

69. Bode, "The Concept of Pure Experience," *op. cit.,* p. 693.

70. A. K. Rogers, "Professor James' Theory of Knowledge," *The Philosophical Review,* XV (November, 1906), 596.

71. Santayana, "Dewey's Naturalistic Metaphysics," *op. cit.,* p. 688.

72. *Ibid.,* p. 685.

73. Spaulding, "A Reply to Professor Dewey's Rejoinder," *op. cit.,* p. 573.

74. Edward Gleason Spaulding, "Realism: A Reply to Professor Dewey and an Exposition," *Journal of Philosophy,* VIII (February 3, 1911), 71.

75. *Ibid.,* pp. 75, 76. Morris Cohen says it is a good "Aristotelian insight that what is prior in knowledge need not be prior in nature." Morris Raphael Cohen, "The New Realism," *Journal of Philosophy,* X (April 10, 1913), 201.

76. Spaulding, "Realism: A Reply to Professor Dewey and an Exposition," *op. cit.,* p. 72. In an attempt to find common ground with Dewey, Spaulding, however, will accept the following: "While the subsistent does not modify cognitively speaking, the existent to which it refers, the act of assertion, which is existential, operates to bring about

171

a transformation into a more desirable form of the existent referred to. Thus, indirectly, a proposition is a medium of a practical, non-cognitive alteration of the thing referred to in knowledge." "Joint Discussion with Articles of Agreement and Disagreement: Professor Dewey and Dr. Spaulding," *Journal of Philosophy*, VIII (October 12, 1911), 577.

77. Arthur O. Lovejoy, "Time, Meaning and Transcendence," *Journal of Philosophy*, XIX (September 14, 28, 1922), 515.

78. Lovejoy, "Pragmatism as Interactionism," *op. cit.*, 623.

79. *Ibid.*, p. 628.

80. Lovejoy, "Time, Meaning and Transcendence," *op. cit.*, 538.

81. Arthur O. Lovejoy, "Pastness and Transcendence," *Journal of Philosophy*, XXI (October 23, 1924), 609.

82. An example of Lovejoy's attempts to assert this dualism of mental and physical and to therefore preserve the fact of an *a priori* structure effecting the physical everyday world is his discussion in *The Revolt against Dualism* (New York: W. W. Norton & Co. Inc., 1930), pp. 291, 292, asserting that it is not "knowing" that affects the object known but rather it is "the action of a certain physical process or instrument upon a certain physical entity." The point rather is, according to Dewey, that what does appear and what would not have appeared would not have been such without the organic activity involved because of the knowing process. In other words, the organic activity due to the knowing process does change the object of knowledge. See Charles W. Morris, *Six Theories of Mind* (Chicago: University of Chicago Press, 1932), p. 306.

83. Lovejoy, "Time, Meaning and Transcendence," *op. cit.*, 511.

84. Santayana, "Dewey's Naturalistic Metaphysics," *op. cit.*, 686.

85. See, for example, Lovejoy, "The Thirteen Pragmatisms," *op. cit.*, 6, 7. Cohen also agrees in his interesting polar way: "Value and historical existence are independent of each other in the same sense that two blades which form a pair of scissors are independent of each other. Both are necessary and intimately connected, but neither can absorb or, by a process of sublimation (*aufhebung*), transcend the other." Cohen, *Reason & Nature,* p. 385.

86. Lovejoy, "Pastness and Transcendence," *op. cit.*, 603; Arthur O. Lovejoy, "Reflections of a Temporalist on the New Realism," *Journal of Philosophy*, VIII (October 26, 1911), 694.

87. McGilvary, "Pure Experience and Reality," *op. cit.*, p. 275.

88. Josiah Royce, *William James and Other Essays* (New York: The Macmillan Company, 1911), p. 232.

89. W. P. Montague, "May a Realist Be a Pragmatist: Implications of Psychological Pragmatism," *Journal of Philosophy*, VI (September 30, 1909), 548. See also Royce, *William James and Other Essays*, p. 215.

90. Perry, "A Review of Pragmatism as a Theory of Knowledge," *op. cit.*, p. 372.

91. *Ibid.*, p. 421.

92. *Ibid.*, pp. 366, 372, 374, 422, 426. See also A. W. Moore, "Professor Perry on Pragmatism," *Journal of Philosophy*, IV (October 10, 1907), 571.

93. Charles M. Bakewell, "Review of W. James' Pragmatism," *The Philosophical Review,* XVI (November, 1907), 633.

94. McGilvary, "Pure Experience and Reality," *op. cit.*, p. 235.

95. John Russell, "Some Difficulties with the Epistemology of Pragmatism and Radical Empiricism," *op. cit.*, p. 410. See also James Bissett Pratt, "Truth & Ideas," *Journal of Philosophy,* V (1908), 122-131. Even Professor Woodbridge

is forced to assert that "truth is not 'that which works' but something in Nature that is worked with." *An Essay on Nature,* p. 47.

96. Edwin Arthur Burtt, "Two Basic Issues in the Problem of Meaning and of Truth," *Essays in Honor of John Dewey* (New York: Henry Holt & Company, 1929), p. 74.

97. Royce, "The Eternal and the Practical," *op. cit.,* p. 139.

98. *Ibid.,* p. 129.

99. *Ibid.,* p. 135.

NOTES FOR CHAPTER III

1. Lovejoy, "Pragmatism as Interactionism," *op. cit.,* p. 631.

2. William James, *The Meaning of Truth* (New York: Longmans, Green, and Co., 1909), XII.

3. William James, *Essays in Radical Empiricism,* p. 160.

4. By this I mean only to imply that "experience" may mean different things with different philosophers. For instance, James' statement that "no one believes more strongly than I do that what our senses know as 'this world' is only one portion of our minds' total environment and object. Yet, because it is the primal portion, it is the *sine qua non* of all the rest. If you grasp the facts about it firmly, you may proceed to higher regions undisturbed," may be hard to accept if you consider experience in somewhat more narrow terms. William James, *Talks to Teachers on Psychology: and to Students on Some of Life's Ideals* (New York: Henry Holt and Co., 1899), p. 25.

5. William James, *Pragmatism,* p. 49.

6. *Ibid.,* p. 45.

7. William James, *Some Problems of Philosophy* (New York: Longmans, Green, and Co., 1911), p. 100. James claims that his philosophy "agrees with nominalism for instance, in always appealing to particulars; with utilitarian-

ism in emphasizing practical aspects; with positivism in its disdain for verbal solutions, useless questions and metaphysical abstractions." *Pragmatism*, p. 53.

8. James, *Essays in Radical Empiricism*, p. 251.

9. James, *Some Problems of Philosophy*, p. 100.

10. William James, *The Will to Believe and Other Essays in Popular Philosophy* (New York: Longmans, Green, and Co., 1912), VII.

11. James, *Some Problems of Philosophy*, p. 198.

12. William James, *The Principles of Psychology* (New York: Henry Holt and Co., 1890), I, 353.

13. William James, *Collected Essays and Reviews*, ed. Ralph Barton Perry (New York: Longmans, Green, and Co., 1920), p. 437.

14. James, *Pragmatism*, p. 86.

15. James, *The Principles of Psychology*, I, 347. This rejection of abstract entities which claim an *a priori* existence does not mean James rejects all concepts of unity. For James this would be running against the entire sense of mankind, of which, for instance, the distinct concept of self seems to be an integral part. Common sense protests against the notion that the bare existence of disconnected phenomena is the total truth by making the claim that the more than the phenomena is "substance" or "soul." It of course explains nothing but it does give concrete form to the belief that the coming of this mind, or personal consciousness, or substance, has some sort of ground in the nature of things. These concepts of unity simply acknowledge the fact that there are different series of experiences that run together by certain definite transactions. Thus James rejects them as ontological substances but accepts them as expressions of this fact.

16. William James, "The Experience of Activity," *The Psychological Review*, XII (1905), 14.

17. William James, *A Pluralistic Universe* (New York: Longmans, Green, and Co., 1909), p. 306.

18. James, *Essays in Radical Empiricism*, pp. 44, 62, 107.

19. James, *Pragmatism*, p. 212.

20. James, *The Principles of Psychology*, I, 240.

21. *Ibid.*, p. 255.

22. *Ibid.*, p. 561. Despite the later complications associated with the term "external relation" I still prefer to use it because it expresses James' meaning very simply. He himself used the term in technical discussion. See *Essays in Radical Empiricism*, pp. 44, 110.

23. James, *Some Problems of Philosophy*, pp. 139, 214.

24. James, *The Will to Believe and Other Essays in Popular Philosophy*, p. 158.

25. James, *Some Problems of Philosophy*, p. 145.

26. *Ibid.*, p. 139.

27. James, *The Principles of Psychology*, II, 619; and James, *The Will to Believe and Other Essays in Popular Philosophy*, VIII.

Perhaps a comment about pluralism is in order. It "means only that the sundry parts of reality may be externally related." That is, it asserts the relations are not intrinsic to the terms related and that, therefore, new relations are possible. In order to make this clearer in the context of a stream of consciousness he says that the connections within the stream exist in a distributive sense rather than in a collective sense. Some of the connections are so loosely effected that some parts in the stream are only associated by "nothing but the copula and. They might even come and go without those other parts suffering any internal change." The stream of consciousness is a "strung along type." The parts are never totally collected and some parts forever remain outside the largest collection of an all. See James, *A Pluralistic Universe*, 34, 321; *Pragmatism*, 139, 66; *Some Problems of Philosophy*, 114, 170; *Essays in Radical Empiricism*, 110.

28. James, *Essays in Radical Empiricism*, 134.

29. *Ibid.*, p. 137.

30. *Ibid.*, p. 23.

31. James, *The Principles of Psychology*, I, 489.

32. James, *Essays in Radical Empiricism*, 86.

33. The term is Perry's. See Ralph Barton Perry, *The Thought and Character of William James* (London: Oxford University Press, 1935), I, 525.

34. James, *Collected Essays and Reviews*, 451. The world is One in that "all things cohere and adhere to each other . . . but just as definitely it is not one." It is "One just so far as we experience it to be concatenated, One by as many definite conjunctions as appear. But then also not One by just as many disjunctions as we find. The oneness and the manyness of it thus obtain respects which can be separately named." James, *Pragmatism*, 137.

35. James, *Some Problems of Philosophy*, 49; *Pragmatism*, 264.

36. James, *Collected Essays and Reviews*, 205; *The Meaning of Truth*, 175.

37. James, *The Principles of Psychology*, I, 488.

38. *Ibid.*, 493, 553; *The Meaning of Truth*, 172, 174; "The Experience of Activity," *op. cit.*, 4. This assertion of natural kinds is essential. "We can easily conceive that every fact in the world might be singular, that is, unlike any other fact and sole of its kind. In such a world of singulars our logic would be useless, for logic works by predicating of the single instances what is true of all its kind. With no two things alike in the world, we should be unable to reason from our past experiences to our future ones. The existence of so much generic unity in things is thus perhaps the most momentous pragmatic specification of what it may mean to say 'the world is one.'" James, *Pragmatism*, 139.

39. James, *The Principles of Psychology*, II, 668.

40. James, *Pragmatism*, 244.

41. "My article spoke vaguely of a 'most chaotic pure experience' coming first, and building up the mind. But how can true structureless things interact so as to produce a structure? my critic triumphantly asks. Of course they can't,

as surely so-named entities. We must make additional hypothesis. We must beg a minimum of structure for them. The kind of minimum that might have intended to increase towards what we now find actually developed is the philosophical desideratum here. The question is that of the most materially satisfactory hypothesis." James, *Essays in Radical Empiricism,* 257.

42. James, *The Principles of Psychology,* II, 677.

43. James, *Collected Essays and Reviews,* 451.

44. James, *The Principles of Psychology,* II, 634.

45. James, *Collected Essays and Reviews,* 501.

46. James, *Essays in Radical Empiricism,* 4.

47. James, *Some Problems of Philosophy,* 113.

48. *Ibid.,* 97.

49. By specifying perception as distinct from sensation James means to include the consciousness of further facts associated with the objects of sensation. But the important thing to note is that he presents facts as an immediately present outward reality. Here again is the empirical movement from parts to wholes, the treatment of the past as fundamental in the order of knowledge as well as in the order of being. James, *The Principles of Psychology,* II, 77, 1-6; *Some Problems of Philosophy,* 98.

50. James, *Some Problems of Philosophy,* 64.

51. James, *Talks to Teachers on Psychology: and to Students on Some of Life's Ideals,* 24.

52. James, *Essays in Radical Empiricism,* 96.

53. James, *Some Problems of Philosophy,* 51.

54. James, *Pragmatism,* 57.

55. James, *Some Problems of Philosophy,* 199.

56. *Ibid.,* 64.

57. James, *The Principles of Psychology,* II, 641.

58. *Ibid.,* I, 467.

59. James, *A Pluralistic Universe,* 286.

60. James, *Pragmatism,* 263.

61. James, *Some Problems of Philosophy,* 75. It is the

"tender minded" approach to the world, relying on principle as contrasted to the "tough minded" approach which relies on "fact." See James, *Pragmatism*, 12.

62. James, *Some Problems of Philosophy*, 86.

63. Perry, *The Thought and Character of William James*, II, 596.

64. James, *Some Problems of Philosophy*, 50.

65. James, *The Principles of Psychology*, II, 636.

66. James, *Collected Essays and Reviews*, 67.

67. *Ibid.*, 80.

68. James, *Pragmatism*, 255.

69. James, *The Principles of Psychology*, I, 402.

70. *Ibid.*, I, 482.

71. *Ibid.*, I, 288. Even though it may not be necessary to say it, this quotation applies to our private ends. "The statue stood there from eternity." In the sense that it did, to this extent it controls us. To this extent James is a realist. "The terms of which that universe consists, positively forbid any non-realistic interpretation of the function of knowledge defined there. The pragmatic epistemologist posits there a reality and a mind with ideas." James, *The Meaning of Truth*, 190.

72. I see no reason why I couldn't have used as an example, James' discussion about the other two traditional ideas, beauty and goodness. He explicitly puts them into a pragmatic context with the statement that "although a value is in one sense an objective quality perceived, the essence of that quality is its relation to the will, and consists in its being a dynamogenic spur that makes our action different." James, *A Pluralistic Universe*, 341. In other words value derives ultimately from being needed or desired. The concepts good, bad, and obligation have no absolute nature independent of personal support. Rather they are objects of feeling and desire which have no foothold or anchorage in being apart from the existence of actually living minds. "The essence of good is simply to satisfy demand. . . . That act

179

must be the best act, accordingly which makes for the best whole, in the sense of awakening the least sum of dissatisfactions." James, *The Will to Believe and Other Essays in Popular Philosophy*, 201-205. I decided on Truth because James spent more time on it, the critics spent more time attacking it, and James himself said that "it seems to me that the establishment of the pragmatist theory of truth is a step of first rate importance in making radical empiricism prevail." James, *The Meaning of Truth*, XII.

73. James, *Pragmatism*, 200.

74. James, *The Meaning of Truth*, 205.

75. James, *Pragmatism*, 192.

76. James, *Collected Essays and Reviews*, 448.

77. James, *The Meaning of Truth*, 75.

78. *Ibid.*, 179.

79. *Ibid.*, 269.

80. *Ibid.*, 100. The background or the facts of a given situation that must verify a particular idea are in another situation ideas themselves. This is in essence Dewey's situational setting. "We all cease analyzing the world at some point, and notice no more differences. The last units with which we stop are our objective elements of being. Those of a dog are different from those of Humboldt; those of a practical man from those of a metaphysician. But the dog's and the practical man's thoughts feel continuous, though to the Humboldt or to the metaphysician they would appear full of gaps and defects and they are continuous, as thought. It is only as mirrors of things that the superior minds find them full of omissions. And when the omitted things are discovered and the unnoticed differences laid bare, it is not that the old thoughts split up, but that new thoughts supersede them, which make new judgments about the same objective world." James, *The Principles of Psychology*, I, 489.

81. James, *A Pluralistic Universe*, 213. See also *The Meaning of Truth*, 244.

82. Perry, *The Thought and Character of William James*, II, 450.

83. James, *The Meaning of Truth*, XVI.

84. William James, *The Letters of William James*, ed. Henry James (Boston: The Atlantic Monthly Press, 1920), II, 295.

85. James, *The Meaning of Truth*, 65. This effectively unites the process by which we obtain truth with Truth itself. "The reasons why I find it satisfactory to believe that any idea is true, the how of my arriving at that belief may be among the very reasons why the idea is true in reality." *Ibid.*, 201.

86. Belief and will are thus related because they are concerned with the same possibility and the same reality. The will draws our attention to an object, in effect creates it, and the belief gives it real stature. Or vice versa. We believe what we need to and the will sees to it that it is real. See James, *Collected Essays and Reviews*, 205; *The Principles of Psychology*, II, 283-284, 320, 321; *Talks to Teachers on Psychology: and to Students on Some of Life's Ideals*, 201.

87. James, *Collected Essays and Reviews*, 34.

88. *Ibid.*, 71.

89. "I think that yesterday was a crisis in my life. I finished the first part of Renouvier's second 'Essais' and see no reason why his definition of free will—'the sustaining of a thought *because I choose to* when I might have other thoughts'—need be the definition of an illusion. At any rate, I will assume for the present—until next year—that it is no illusion. My first act of free will shall be to believe in free will." James, *The Letters of William James*, I, 147.

90. James actually uses the word instrument. See *Pragmatism*, 53, 58.

91. James, *Some Problems of Philosophy*, 224.

92. James, *Pragmatism*, 216.

93. James, *The Meaning of Truth*, 235.

94. Perry, *The Thought and Character of William James*, II, 635.

95. James, *Pragmatism*, 80.

96. James, *Collected Essays and Reviews*, 412.

97. James, *The Meaning of Truth*, 163. Practical should not be interpreted in the narrow literal sense. It is synonymous with particular and consequences or experiences can perfectly well be of a theoretical nature as of a physical nature. *Ibid.*, 210, 52.

98. James, *Pragmatism*, 200.

99. James, *The Meaning of Truth*, VI.

100. *Ibid.*, 154.

101. James, *Pragmatism*, 64.

102. James, *Essays in Radical Empiricism*, 251.

103. James, *The Meaning of Truth*, 89.

104. *Ibid.*, 159.

105. Perry, *The Thought and Character of William James*, II, 475.

NOTES FOR CHAPTER IV

1. John Dewey, *Studies in Logical Theory* (Chicago: The University of Chicago Press, 1903), 72. The seriousness of "placing the standard of thought and knowledge in antecedent existence is that our thought makes no difference in what is significantly real. It then affects only our own attitude toward it. This constant throwing of emphasis back upon a change made in ourselves instead of one made in the world in which we live seems to me the essence of what is objectionable in 'subjectivism.'" John Dewey, *The Quest for Certainty* (New York: Minton, Balch & Co., 1929), 275.

2. John Dewey, "Some Implications of Anti-Intellectualism," *Journal of Philosophy*, VII (September 1, 1910), 479.

3. Dewey, "Classicism as an Evangel," *op. cit.*, 666.

4. John Dewey, *Problems of Men* (New York: The Philosophical Library, 1946), 287.

5. Dewey, *Studies in Logical Theory,* 61.

6. John Dewey, *Logic* (New York: Henry Holt & Co., 1938), 139.

7. John Dewey, *Experience and Nature* (2nd ed.; New York: W. W. Norton & Co. Inc., 1929), 50.

8. John Dewey, *Human Nature and Conduct* (New York: The Modern Library edition, 1922), 300.

9. Dewey, *Problems of Men,* 213.

10. Dewey, *Human Nature and Conduct,* 232.

11. Dewey, *Problems of Men,* 8.

12. John Dewey, "The Superstition of Necessity," *Monist,* III (April, 1893), 362.

13. John Dewey, *Essays in Experimental Logic* (Chicago: The University of Chicago Press, 1916), 221.

14. John Dewey, *Reconstruction in Philosophy* (London: University of London Press, 1921), 123.

15. John Dewey, "Philosophy," *Whither Mankind.* ed. Charles A. Beard (New York: Longmans, Green and Co., 1937), 320.

16. Dewey, *Reconstruction in Philosophy,* 113.

17. John Dewey, *The Influence of Darwin on Philosophy* (New York: Henry Holt and Co., 1910), 13.

18. John Dewey, *Characters and Events,* ed. Joseph Ratner (New York: Henry Holt and Company, 1929), I, 64.

19. Dewey, *Problems of Men,* 200.

20. Dewey, *The Quest for Certainty,* 126.

21. Dewey, *Experience and Nature,* 1.

22. John Dewey, "Experience, Knowledge and Value: A Rejoinder," *op. cit.,* 532.

23. John Dewey, *Art as Experience* (New York: Minton, Balch and Company, 1934), 134.

24. Dewey, *The Quest for Certainty,* 243.

25. Dewey, *Art as Experience,* 103.

26. Dewey, "Experience, Knowledge and Value: A Rejoinder," *op. cit.,* 545.

27. Dewey, *Experience and Nature,* 241. Nature is a

rhythmic order, so to speak. It is true that what is form in one context or connection can be matter in another context, yet the labels form and matter do signify different aspects of the rhythmic order. Matter designates something capable of being expressed in mathematical symbols, which are distinguished from those defining energy. It designates a character in operation, change, sequential order, not an entity. "It is no cause or source of events or processes; no absolute monarch; no principle of explanation, no substance behind or underlying changes." *Ibid.,* 73. Rather, it is a condition or means for the existence of something else, it is the precarious in nature and also the continuity in nature. Form on the other hand represents change arrested in a prerogative object. It conveys a sense of the imperishable timeless, and the stable. It thus conveys security and self-possessed order of meaning. Every experienced object in some sense is a closing episode, an end, a desirable consummation of conditions, and this is form. Interest is form because it is responsible for the freezing of change into a particular object. The product is an esthetic experience.

28. Dewey, *The Quest for Certainty,* 210.

29. Dewey, *Human Nature and Conduct,* 150.

30. Dewey, "Experience, Knowledge and Value: A Rejoinder," *op. cit.,* 548.

31. Dewey, *Logic,* 280.

32. Dewey, *Essays in Experimental Logic,* 35. Note too that the initial phase is the non-cognitive situation from which knowing develops, the second or intermediate phase is where the subject matter becomes conditioned by the inquiry, "and hence is tentative, provisional, conditional, pending completion of inquiry," and the terminal or third stage is that of attained knowledge. This third stage is that of the object known, the second stage is the something had in immediate experience that evokes thought. The one is final redisposition of the other. The whole process is intelligent but only the last phase is knowledge. Dewey, "Expe-

rience, Knowledge and Value: A Rejoinder," *op. cit.*, 564-566.

33. "All life has its élan, but only the prevalence of dead habits deflects life into mere élan." Dewey, *Human Nature and Conduct*, 71.

34. ". . . the indispensableness to the instrumentalist theories of truth, even as working empirical theories, of a recognition of the social implications of ideas and beliefs. This indispensableness appears, to Professor Royce, fatal to the instrumental conception; to me it seems its essence." John Dewey, "A Reply to Professor Royce's Critique of Instrumentalism," *The Philosophical Review*, XXI (January, 1912), 69.

35. Dewey, *Art as Experience*, 246.

36. By psychology in the broad sense, I mean the natural history of the various attitudes and structures through which experiencing passes. "It is an account of the conditions under which this or that state emerges, and of the way in which it influences, by stimulation or inhibition, production of other states or conformations of consciousness." Dewey, *Studies in Logical Theory*, 15. By morals in the broad sense, I mean to include "all of the subjects of distinctively human import, all of the social disciplines as far as they are intimately connected with the life of man as they bear upon the interests of humanity." Dewey, *Human Nature and Conduct*, V. Dewey himself accepts these terms in this sense.

37. Dewey, *Human Nature and Conduct*, 195.

38. Dewey, *The Influence of Darwin on Philosophy*, 269.

39. Dewey, *Logic*, 76.

40. Dewey, *Reconstruction in Philosophy*, 177. We may consider philosophy to be the process of inquiry as it passes into reconstructive social and personal action. The moral problem is whether intelligent guidance of the course of life's conduct is possible. It involves the disposition to maintain the integrity of inquiry. Morals and philosophy are interwoven because without the demands of moral integrity

applied to inquiry, the consequence does not verify the hypothesis and the practical does not verify the intellectual. Moral integrity demands that both the organism and the environment be subject to revision "as we find observational data which supply better evidence, and as growth of science provides better directive hypotheses to draw upon." Dewey, *The Quest for Certainty*, 173. The practical and the intellectual are so related that when we imagine we are thinking of an exclusively theoretical doubt, we unconsciously smuggle in some consequence which hangs upon it. This is the practical, a concrete concern with what is to be done, with the future responses which an object requires of us or commits us to. Dewey, *Essays in Experimental Logic*, 323; *The Quest for Certainty*, 39; *Logic*, 160. The business of philosophy is that of morals. It is not to pretend it can speculate upon man's final end and upon an ultimate standard of right and wrong but rather to utilize physiology, anthropology and psychology in order to discover all that can be discovered about man, his organic powers and propensities. The business of morals "is to converge all the instrumentalities of the social arts, of law, education and political science upon the construction of intelligent methods of improving the common lot." Dewey, *The Influence of Darwin on Philosophy*, 69. The business of philosophy is to "become a method of locating and interpreting the more serious of the conflicts that occur in life, and a method of projecting ways for dealing with them: a method of moral and political diagnosis and prognosis. *Ibid.*, 17. "Unless philosophies are to be Edens of compensatory refuge, reached through an exercise of dialectic ingenuity they must face the situation which is there. It is their business to bring intellectual order out of the confusion of beliefs." Dewey, "Philosophy," *op. cit.*, 326. This is why there is a necessity of defining philosophy from the standpoint of value. See John Dewey, "Philosophy," *Encyclopedia of the Social Sciences*, Vol. XII.

41. Dewey, *Logic,* 23.

42. It might be well to say that the need or problem that instigates the process of inquiry is not the same as a personal need or problem unless that personal need in turn founds itself on a situation that is problematic. This is the distinction between the nature of the subject matter inquired into and the attitude of the inquirer. The only personal desire that enters into this situation is a desire to resolve as honestly and impartially as possible the problem involved in the situation. Dewey, *Problems of Men,* 200; "Experience, Knowledge and Value: A Rejoinder," *op. cit.,* 572, 582, 587.

43. Dewey, *Human Nature and Conduct,* 249; *The Quest for Certainty,* 244; *The Influence of Darwin on Philosophy,* 127, 299.

44. Dewey, *Essays in Experimental Logic,* 301.

45. See John Dewey, "The Realism of Pragmatism," *Journal of Philosophy,* II (June 8, 1905).

46. "This question takes us to the matter of whether there are ultimate, that is, irreducible, traits of the very existences with which scientific reflection is concerned. [He says there are.] . . . Accordingly, they would seem to deserve the name of ultimate, or irreducible, traits. As such they may be made the object of a kind of inquiry differing from that which deals with the genesis of a particular group of existences, a kind of inquiry to which the name metaphysical may be given." John Dewey, "The Subject-Matter of Metaphysical Inquiry," *Journal of Philosophy,* XII (June 24, 1915), 339.

47. Dewey, *Art as Experience,* 120.

48. Dewey, *Experience and Nature,* 96.

49. Dewey, *The Influence of Darwin on Philosophy,* 259.

50. Dewey, *Logic,* 273. See also *Experience and Nature,* 182.

51. Dewey, *Problems of Men,* 185, 217, 226, 241, 246.

52. Dewey, *Logic,* 168; *Problems of Men,* 228.

53. Dewey, *Problems of Men,* 247.

54. Dewey, "Philosophy," *Whither Mankind,* 330.

55. Dewey, *The Quest for Certainty,* 94.

56. *Ibid.,* 133.

57. Dewey, *Art as Experience,* 73. I don't want to imply that Dewey slights in any way the role of art. When an object is perceived for what it is without the need for reflective inquiry, the quality is what it means, the object to which it belongs. Art has the faculty of enhancing and concentrating this union of quality and meaning in a way which vivifies both. Instead of canceling a separation between sense and meaning it exemplifies in an accentuated and perfected manner the union characteristic of many other experiences, through finding the exact qualitative media that fuse most completely with what is to be expressed. *Ibid.,* 259. In so far as the process of inquiry projects method and relations for the future it is the artistic process and its end product, the concretely experienced qualitative object is a product of art. In fact, everything we know is a product of art, our philosophies, our religions, as well as our methods and objects. Dewey, *The Quest for Certainty,* 125. For interesting reading see J. H. Randall, Jr., "Instrumentalism and Mythology," *op. cit.*

58. Its end product is an object of art as defined above. Its objective of unification is the reason why it has moral and philosophical significance. John Dewey, "The Evolutionary Method as Applied to Morality," *The Philosophical Review, XI* (July, 1902), 370.

59. Dewey, *Reconstruction in Philosophy,* 135.

60. "I too, conceive that things had in direct experience exist prior to being known. But I deny the identity of things had in direct experience with the object of knowledge *qua* object of knowledge. Things that are had in experience exist prior to reflection and its eventuation in an object of knowledge; but the latter, as such is a deliberately effected re-arrangement or re-disposition, by means of overt operations,

of such antecedent existences." John Dewey, "In Reply to Some Criticisms," *Journal of Philosophy*, XXVII (May 8, 1930), 273.

61. Dewey, *Logic*, 133.

62. *Ibid.*, 491; Dewey, *The Quest for Certainty*, 138, 168, 288.

63. Dewey, *Studies in Logical Theory*, 65; *Art as Experience*, 118.

64. John Dewey, "Pure Experience and Reality: A Declaimer," *The Philosophical Review*, XVI (July, 1907), 421.

65. John Dewey, "Realism without Monism or Dualism," *Journal of Philosophy*, XIX (June 22, 1922), 358.

66. Dewey, *Experience and Nature*, 158.

67. Dewey, *Art as Experience*, 272.

68. Dewey, *Logic*, 461. These universal propositions are of the if-then variety. Therefore they are hypothesis yet to be verified. They are non-existential in import, concerned with possible operations. Generic propositions differ in that they have existential reference. The relation is something akin to science and philosophy. The universal if-then proposition determines whether or not the generic proposition is possible. As such it is an expression of the structural aspect of nature, but remember again that this structure is functional. Generic and universal propositions represent cooperative divisions in the inquiry which transform problematic situations into resolved and unified ones. *Ibid.*, 272-280, 381, 264.

69. *Ibid.*, 269, 271-279, 317, 454.

70. *Ibid.*, 3.

71. *Ibid.*, 386.

72. Dewey, "Realism without Monism or Dualism," *op. cit.*, 309. See also John Dewey, "Some Comments on Philosophical Discussion," *Journal of Philosophy*, XXI (April 10, 1924), 197-209.

73. I believe this is an especially important point to make explicit. First, Dewey asserts that there is an ante-

cedent reality to that reality known. In a letter to James he said, "I have repeated *ad nauseam* that there are existences prior to and subsequent to cognitive states and purposes." Perry, *The Thought and Character of William James,* II, 532. I agree. The business of thought is always to reconstruct, never to create. Second, Dewey makes a distinction between the antecedent and the object known. Dewey, "Some Comments on Philosophical Discussion," *op. cit.,* 199; "Experience, Knowledge and Value: A Rejoinder," *op. cit.,* 548. Third, this antecedent to the object known, termed "subject matter" (Dewey, "Some Comments on Philosophical Discussion," *op. cit.,* 206) undergoes reconstruction, not the object of knowledge. Dewey, "In Reply to Some Criticism," *op. cit.,* 273; "Experience, Knowledge and Value: A Rejoinder," *op. cit.,* 547; Donald A. Piatt, "Dewey's Logical Theory," *The Philosophy of John Dewey,* ed. Paul Arthur Schillp ("The Library of Living Philosophers"; New York: Tudor Publishing Company, 1939), 129. Fourth, when the object of knowledge is finally constituted there is no object standing apart from the subject matter but the antecedent and the object are one. John Dewey, "An Empirical Account of Appearance," *Journal of Philosophy,* XXIV (August 18, 1927), 458.

74. Dewey, *The Quest for Certainty,* 204.

75. Dewey, *Logic,* 215; *Art as Experience,* 217. If philosophy is to contribute to the solving of humanity's ills the leading of the process of inquiry to a new concentration of quantity and quality should not be too surprising.

76. Dewey, "Experience, Knowledge and Value: A Rejoinder," *op. cit.,* 521.

77. James, *Pragmatism,* 201.

78. Dewey, "A Reply to Professor Royce's Critique of Instrumentalism," *op. cit.,* 75.

79. "Satisfaction is satisfaction of the conditions prescribed by the problem. Personal satisfaction may enter in as it arises when any job is well done according to the re-

quirements of the job itself; but it does not enter in any way into the determination of validity, because on the contrary it is conditioned by that determination." Dewey, "Experience, Knowledge and Value: A Rejoinder," *op. cit.*, 572.

80. Dewey, *Human Nature and Conduct*, 211. See John Herman Randall, Jr., "Dualism in Metaphysics and Practical Philosophy," *Essays in Honor of John Dewey* (New York: Henry Holt and Company, 1929), 318.

81. Dewey, *Problems of Men*, 157.

82. Dewey, *Essays in Experimental Logic*, 361.

83. See John Dewey, "The Objects of Valuation," *Journal of Philosophy*, XV (May 9, 1918), 253-258.

84. The object of knowledge is to redirect natural processes, and the object of knowledge is ultimately found among such redirected processes. For Dewey, the implications of this fully agree with the findings of science: that the characters of things are not absolute but relative, that the characters given in perceptual experience are dependent on physical conditions varying with the diverse relations of perceivers to the object, and upon the special constitution of the perceiver or knower. See Morris, *Six Theories of Mind*, 307; and John Dewey, "Substance, Power, and Quality in Locke," *The Philosophical Review*, XXXV (January, 1926), 23.

Notes for Postscript

1. George Santayana, *The Life of Reason* (One Volume ed.; New York: Charles Scribner's Sons, 1955), 285.

2. This is based in part on the simple principle that if a theme recurs enough it must have some validity. More technically, it is based on the intrinsic relationship between a theory of knowledge and the theory of nature. "The difference between them would not be a difference in subject-matter, but a difference in attention. The exhibition

of the principles which govern the understanding in attempting to gain a comprehensive view of nature would be a theory of knowledge. It would also be a theory of nature because those principles would exhibit characters of nature by which the understanding is governed and without which the attempt to understand would not itself be understood." Woodbridge, *Nature and Mind*, 277. "No science can be more secure than the unconscious metaphysics which tacitly it presupposes. The individual thing is necessarily a modification of its environment, and cannot be understood in disjunction. All reasoning, apart from some metaphysical reference, is vicious." Alfred North Whitehead, *Adventure of Ideas* (New York: The Macmillan Company, 1933), 197.

3. "If one will talk of needs, the need of speech is like the need of food—not a desire which comes first and then creates organs and manipulates circumstances in order to realize the desire, but a consequence of having those organs and of their cooperation with the circumstances in which they are exercised. A creature without a digestive system would have no need of food; one without voice organs would have no need of speech. Furthermore, a creature with a digestive system would starve in a world where there was no food; one with vocal cords would have nothing to say in a world where sounds had no expressive effect." Woodbrige, *An Essay on Nature*, 226.

4. Ernest Nagel, "Can Logic Be Divorced from Ontology," *Journal of Philosophy*, XVI (December 19, 1929), 708.

BIBLIOGRAPHY

This bibliography represents books which I have used. I do not intend it to be exhaustive.

Adams, G. P. "Activity and Objects in Dewey's Human Nature & Conduct," *Journal of Philosophy*, XX (October 25, 1923), 596-603.

Angell, James Rowland. "The Relations of Structural & Functional Psychology to Philosophy," *The Philosophical Review*, XII (May, 1903), 243-70.

"Apollo," *Encyclopaedia Britannica*, Vol. I, 11th edition.

Apollodorus. *The Library*. Translated by James George Frazer. London: William Heinemann, 1921.

"Apostolic Fathers, The." *The Fathers of the Church*. Edited by Ludwig Schopp, *et al.* New York: Cima Publishing Co., 1946.

Augustine. "De Trinitate," *A Select Library of the Nicene and Post Nicene Fathers*. Edited by Philip Schaff. First Series. Buffalo: Christian Literature Company, 1887.

"Baal," *Encyclopaedia Britannica*, Vol. II, 1955 edition.

Bakewell, Charles M. "Review of William James' Pragmatism," *The Philosophical Review*, XVI (November, 1907), 624-34.

Basil. "Select Works and Letters," *A Select Library of the Nicene and Post Nicene Fathers*. Edited by Philip

Schaff, *et al.* Vol. VIII. Second Series. New York: Christian Literature Company, 1895.

Bixler, Julius Seelye. *Religion in the Philosophy of William James.* Boston: Marshall Jones Company, 1926.

Bode, B. H. "Cognitive Experience and Its Object," *Journal of Philosophy*, II (November 23, 1905), 658-63.

————. "The Concept of Pure Experience," *The Philosophical Review*, XIV (November, 1905), 684-95.

————. "Intelligence & Behavior," *Journal of Philosophy*, XVIII (January 6, 1921), 10-17.

Brown, Harold Chapman. "Review of Dewey's Essays in Experimental Logic," *Journal of Philosophy*, XIV (April 26, 1917), 246-48.

Bush, Wendell T. "The Background of Instrumentalism," *Journal of Philosophy*, XX (December 20, 1923), 701-14.

————. "Constructive Intelligence," *Journal of Philosophy*, XIV (September 13, 1917), 505-20.

————. "The Problem of the 'Ego-Centric Predicament,'" *Journal of Philosophy*, VIII (August 3, 1911), 438-39.

Carter, Jesse B. *The Religion of Numa.* New York: Macmillan Co., 1906.

Cochrane, Charles Norris. *Christianity and Classical Culture.* New York: Oxford University Press, 1944.

Cohen, Morris R. "The Conception of Philosophy in Recent Discussion," *Journal of Philosophy*, VII (July 21, 1910), 401-10.

————. "The Distinction Between the Mental & the Physical," *Journal of Philosophy*, XIV (May 10, 1917), 261-67.

————. "The New Realism," *Journal of Philosophy*, X (April 10, 1913), 197-214.

————. *Reason & Nature.* New York: Harcourt, Brace & Company, 1931.

Complete Greek Drama, The. Edited by Whitney Oates and Eugene O'Neill, Jr. 2 vols. New York: Random House, 1938.

Cornford, F. M. *Greek Religious Thought*. London: J. M. Dent & Sons, Ltd., 1923.

Cumont, Franz. *The Oriental Religions in Roman Paganism*. Chicago: The Open Court Publishing Company, 1911.

Dewey, John. "An Analysis of Reflective Thought," *Journal of Philosophy*, XIX (January 19, 1922), 29-38.

———. "Antinaturalism in Extremis," *Naturalism and the Human Spirit*. Edited by Yervant H. Krikorian. New York: Columbia University Press, 1944, 1-16.

———. "The Applicability of Logic to Existence," *Journal of Philosophy*, XXVII (March 27, 1930), 174-79.

———. *Art as Experience*. New York: Minton Balch and Company, 1934.

———. *Characters and Events*. Edited by Joseph Ratner. 2 vols. New York: Henry Holt and Company, 1929.

———. "Classicism as an Evangel," *Journal of Philosophy*, XVIII (November 24, 1921), 664-66.

———. "The Concept of the Neutral in Recent Epistemology," *Journal of Philosophy*, XIV (March 15, 1917), 161-63.

———. "Concerning Alleged Immediate Knowledge of Mind," *Journal of Philosophy*, XV (January 17, 1918), 29-35.

———. "Concerning Novelties in Logic: A Reply to Mr. Robinson," *Journal of Philosophy*, XIV (April 26, 1917), 237-45.

———. "The Dilemma of the Intellectualist Theory of Truth," *Journal of Philosophy*, VI (August 5, 1909), 433-34.

———. "Duality & Dualism," *Journal of Philosophy*, XIV (August 30, 1917), 491-93.

———. "An Empirical Account of Appearance," *Journal of Philosophy*, XXIV (August 18, 1927), 449-63.

———. *Essays in Experimental Logic*. Chicago: The University of Chicago Press, 1916.

————. "The Evolutionary Method as Applied to Morality," *The Philosophical Review*, XI (March, July, 1902), 107-24; 353-71.

————. *Experience and Nature*. New York: W. W. Norton & Co., Inc., 1929.

————. "Experience, Knowledge and Value: A Rejoinder," *The Philosophy of John Dewey*. Edited by Paul Arthur Schillip. "The Library of Living Philosophers." New York: Tudor Publishing Company, 1939.

————. "Half-Hearted Naturalism," *Journal of Philosophy*, XXIV (February 3, 1927), 57-64.

————. *Human Nature and Conduct*. New York: The Modern Library Edition, 1922.

————. "Immediate Empiricism," *Journal of Philosophy*, II (October 26, 1905), 597-99.

————. *The Influence of Darwin on Philosophy*. New York: Henry Holt and Co., 1910.

————. "Joint Discussion with Articles of Agreement and Disagreement: Professor Dewey and Dr. Spaulding," *Journal of Philosophy*, VIII (October 12, 1911), 574-79.

————. "The Knowledge Experience Again," *Journal of Philosophy*, II (December 21, 1905), 707-11.

————. "The Knowledge Experience & Its Relationships," *Journal of Philosophy*, II (November 23, 1905), 652-57.

————. *Logic*. New York: Henry Holt & Co., 1938.

————. "Meaning and Existence," *Journal of Philosophy*, XXV (June 21, 1928), 345-53.

————. "The Naturalistic Theory of Perception by the Senses," *Journal of Philosophy*, XXII (October 22, 1925), 596-605.

————. "Notes Upon Logical Topics: I. A Classification of Contemporary Tendencies; II. The Meanings of the Term 'Idea,'" *Journal of Philosophy*, I (February 4, March 31, 1904), 57-62; 175-78.

————. "Objects, Data, & Existences: A Reply to Professor

McGilvary," *Journal of Philosophy,* VI (January 7, 1909), 13-21.

—————. "The Objects of Valuation," *Journal of Philosophy,* XV (May 9, 1918), 253-58.

—————. "Perception & Organic Action," *Journal of Philosophy,* IX (November 21, 1912), 645-68.

—————. "Philosophy," *Whither Mankind.* Edited by Charles A. Beard. New York: Longmans, Green and Co., 1937.

—————. "Philosophy," *Encyclopedia of the Social Sciences.* Vol. 12, 1935.

—————. "Philosophy," *Research in the Social Sciences.* Edited by Wilson Gee. New York: Macmillan Co., 1929, 241-65.

—————. "The Postulate of Immediate Empiricism," *Journal of Philosophy,* II (July 20, 1905), 393-99.

—————. "The Pragmatism of Peirce," *Journal of Philosophy,* XIII (December 21, 1916), 709-15.

—————. *Problems of Men.* New York: Philosophical Library, 1946.

—————. *Psychology.* 3rd ed. revised. New York: American Book Company, 1891.

—————. "Pure Experience & Reality: A Disclaimer," *The Philosophical Review,* XVI (July, 1907), 419-22.

—————. *The Quest for Certainty.* New York: Minton, Balch & Company, 1929.

—————. "The Realism of Pragmatism," *Journal of Philosophy,* II (June 8, 1905), 324-27.

—————. "Realism without Monism or Dualism," *Journal of Philosophy,* XIX (June 8, 22, 1922), 309-17; 351-61.

—————. "Reality As Experience," *Journal of Philosophy,* III (May 10, 1906), 253-57.

—————. *Reconstruction in Philosophy.* London: University of London Press, 1921.

—————. "Rejoinder to Dr. Spaulding," *Journal of Philosophy,* VIII (February 3, 1911), 77-79.

197

————. "A Reply to Professor Royce's Critique of Instrumentalism," *The Philosophical Review*, XXI (January, 1912), 69-81.

————. "In Reply to Some Criticism," *Journal of Philosophy*, XXVII (May 8, 1930), 271-77.

————. "In Response to Professor McGilvary," *Journal of Philosophy*, IX (September 26, 1912), 544-48.

————. "The Short Cut to Realism Examined," *Journal of Philosophy*, VII (September 29, 1910), 553-57.

————. "Some Comments on Philosophical Discussion," *Journal of Philosophy*, XXI (April 10, 1924), 197-209.

————. "Some Implications of Anti-Intellectualism," *Journal of Philosophy*, VII (September 1, 1910), 477-81.

————. "The Sphere of Application of the Excluded Middle," *Journal of Philosophy*, XXVI (December 19, 1929), 701-05.

————. *Studies in Logical Theory*. Chicago: The University of Chicago Press, 1903.

————. "The Subject-Matter of Metaphysical Inquiry," *Journal of Philosophy*, XII (June 24, 1915), 337-45.

————. "Substance, Power and Quality in Locke," *The Philosophical Review*, XXXV (January, 1926), 22-38.

————. "The Superstition of Necessity," *Monist*, III (April, 1893), 362-79.

————. "The Terms 'Conscious' and 'Consciousness,'" *Journal of Philosophy*, III (January 18, 1906), 39-41.

————. "Valid Knowledge and the 'Subjectivity of Experience,'" *Journal of Philosophy*, VII (March 31, 1910), 169-74.

————. "Values, Liking and Thought," *Journal of Philosophy*, XX (November 8, 1923), 617-22.

————. "William James as Empiricist," *In Commemoration of William James*. Edited by H. M. Kallen. New York: Columbia University Press, 1942, 48-57.

Dodds, E. R. *The Greeks and the Irrational*. Los Angeles: The University of California Press, 1956.

Drake, Durant. "Dr. Dewey's Duality & Dualism," *Journal of Philosophy*, XIV (November 22, 1917), 660-63.

Essays in Honor of John Dewey. New York: Henry Holt & Company, 1929.

Euripides. "Bacchae," *The Complete Greek Drama*. Translated by Gilbert Murray. New York: Random House, 1938. II, 216, 234.

Feldman, W. T. *The Philosophy of John Dewey*. Baltimore: The Johns Hopkins Press, 1934.

Gaster, Theodore H. "Ba'al is Risen," *Iraq*, VI (Autumn, 1939), Part 2, 109-43.

———. "The Religion of the Canaanites," *Forgotten Religions*. Edited by Vergilius Ferm. New York: The Philosophical Library, 1950.

———. *Thespis*. New York: Henry Schuman, 1950.

Grant, Frederick C. *Hellenistic Religions*. New York: The Liberal Arts Press, 1953.

Gregory of Nazianzus. "Select Works and Letters," *A Select Library of Nicene and Post-Nicene Fathers*. Edited by Philip Schaff, *et al.* Second Series. Vol. VIII. New York: Christian Literature Company, 1895.

———. "Theological Orations," *Christology of the Later Fathers*. Edited by Edward R. Hardy. Vol. III of the "Library of Christian Classics." Philadelphia: Westminster Press, 1954.

Gregory of Nyssa. "Address on Religious Instruction," and on "Not Three Gods," *Christology of the Later Fathers*. Edited by Edward R. Hardy. Vol. III of the "Library of Christian Classics." Philadelphia: Westminster Press, 1954.

———. "Select Works of," *A Select Library of Nicene and Post-Nicene Fathers*. Edited by Philip Schaff, *et al.* Vol. V. Second Series. New York: Christian Literature Company, 1893.

Guthrie, W. K. C. *The Greeks and Their Gods*. London: Methuen & Co., 1950.

————. *Orpheus and Greek Religion*. London: Methuen & Co., 1935.

Harrison, Jane E. *Prolegomena to the Study of Greek Religion*. Cambridge: At the University Press, 1908.

Herodotus. *History*. Translated by A. D. Godley. 4 vols. London: William Heinemann, 1921-1924.

Hesiod. *Theogony*. Translated by Norman C. Brown. New York: The Liberal Arts Press, 1953.

Hibben, John Grier. "The Test of Pragmatism," *The Philosophical Review*, XVII (July, 1908), 365-82.

Hocking, William Ernest. "Action & Certainty," *Journal of Philosophy*, XXVII (April 24, 1930), 225-38.

Homer. *Homeric Hymns*. Translated by Andrew Lang. New York: Longmans, Green & Co., 1899.

————. *The Iliad*. Translated by E. V. Rieu. Harmondsworth, Middlesex: Penguin Books, Ltd., 1950.

————. *The Odyssey*. Translated by E. V. Rieu. Baltimore: Penguin Books, Inc., 1946.

Hook, Sidney. *The Metaphysics of Pragmatism*. Chicago: Open Court Publishing Company, 1927.

James, William. *Collected Essays and Reviews*. Edited by Ralph Barton Perry. New York: Longmans, Green and Co., 1920.

————. *The Energies of Men*. New York: Moffat, Yard & Co., 1908.

————. *Essays in Radical Empiricism*. Edited by Ralph Barton Perry. New York: Longmans, Green and Co., 1912.

————. "The Experience of Activity," *The Psychological Review*, XII (January, 1905).

————. *The Letters of William James*. Edited by Henry James. 2 vols. Boston: The Atlantic Monthly Press, 1920.

————. *The Meaning of Truth*. New York: Longmans, Green and Co., 1929.

————. *A Pluralistic Universe*. New York: Longmans, Green and Co., 1909.

————. *Pragmatism*. New York: Longmans, Green and Co., 1928.

————. *The Principles of Psychology*. 2 vols. New York: Henry Holt and Company, 1890.

————. *Some Problems of Philosophy*. New York: Longmans, Green and Co., 1911.

————. *Talks to Teachers on Psychology: and to Students on Some of Life's Ideals*. New York: Henry Holt and Co., 1899.

————. *The Will to Believe and Other Essays in Popular Philosophy*. New York: Longmans, Green and Co., 1912.

John Dewey, The Man and His Philosophy. Cambridge, Mass.: Harvard University Press, 1930.

Kallen, Horace M. "The Affiliations of Pragmatism," *Journal of Philosophy*, VI (November 25, 1909), 655-61.

Kallen, H. M., ed. *In Commemoration of William James*. New York: Columbia University Press, 1942.

Kantor, J. R. "Instrumental Transformism & the Un-Realities of Realism," *Journal of Philosophy*, XVI (August 14, 1919), 449-61.

Kapelrud, Arvid S. *Baal in the Ras Shamra Texts*. Copenhagen: G.E.C. Gad, 1952.

Krikorian, Yervant H., ed. *Naturalism and the Human Spirit*. New York: Columbia University Press, 1944.

Lamprecht, Sterling P. "A Note on Professor Dewey's Theory of Knowledge," *Journal of Philosophy*, XX (August 30, 1923), 488-94.

LeMarchant, A. *Greek Religion to the Time of Hesiod*. Manchester: Sherratt and Hughes, 1923.

Leslie, Elmer A. *Old Testament Religion*. New York: The Abingdon Press, 1936.

Lewis, C. I. "Pragmatism & Current Thought," *Journal of Philosophy*, XXVII (April 24, 1930), 238-46.

————. "Review of Dewey's The Quest for Certainty," *Journal of Philosophy*, XXVII (January 2, 1930), 14-25.

Lovejoy, Arthur O. "Pastness & Transcendence," *Journal of Philosophy*, XXI (October 23, 1924), 601-11.

————. "Pragmatism & Realism," *Journal of Philosophy*, VI (October 14, 1909), 575-80.

————. "Pragmatism as Interactionism," *Journal of Philosophy*, XVII (October 21, November 4, 1920), 589-96; 622-32.

————. "Present Philosophical Tendencies," *Journal of Philosophy*, IX (November 7, 1912), 627-40.

————. "Reflections of a Temporalist on the New Realism," *Journal of Philosophy*, VIII (October 26, 1911), 589-99.

————. *The Revolt against Dualism*. New York: W. W. Norton & Co., 1930.

————. "The Thirteen Pragmatisms," *Journal of Philosophy*, V (January 2, 16, 1908), 5-12; 29-39.

————. "Time, Meaning and Transcendence," *Journal of Philosophy*, XIX (September 14, 28, 1922), 505-15; 533-41.

Macchioro, Vittorio. *From Orpheus to Paul*. New York: Henry Holt & Co., 1930.

McGilvary, Evander Bradley. "Pure Experience & Reality," *The Philosophical Review*, XVI (May, 1907), 266-84.

Miller, Dickinson, S. "James's Philosophical Development: Professor Perry's Biography," *Journal of Philosophy*, XXXIII (June 4, 1936), 309-18.

Montague, W. P. "May a Realist Be a Pragmatist: I. The Two Doctrines Defined. II. Implications of Instrumentalism. III. Implications of Psychological Pragmatism. IV. Implications of Humanism and of the Pragmatic Criterion," *Journal of Philosophy*, VI (August 19, September 2, 30, October 14, 1909), 460-63; 485-90; 543-48; 561-71.

————. "The New Realism & The Old," *Journal of Philosophy*, IX (January 18, 1912), 39-46.

————. *The Ways of Knowing*. London: George Allen & Unwin Ltd., 1925.

Moore, Addison W. "Pragmatism & Its Critics," *The Philosophical Review*, XIV (May, 1905), 322-43.

————. "Pragmatism & Solipsism," *Journal of Philosophy*, VI (July 8, 1909), 378-83.

———. "Professor Perry on Pragmatism," *Journal of Philosophy*, IV (October 10, 1907), 567-77.

———. "Some Lingering Misconceptions of Instrumentalism," *Journal of Philosophy*, XVII (September 9, 1920), 514-19.

Morris, Charles. *Paths of Life*. New York: Harper & Brothers, 1942.

———. *Six Theories of Mind*. Chicago: University of Chicago Press, 1932.

Nagel, Ernest. "Can Logic Be Divorced from Ontology?" *Journal of Philosophy*, XVI (December 19, 1929), 705-12.

Niebuhr, Reinhold. *The Nature & Destiny of Man*. 2 vols. New York: Charles Scribner's Sons, 1948.

Nietzsche, Friedrich. *The Philosophy of Nietzsche*. New York: The Modern Library, 1927.

Nilsson, Martin. *Greek Piety*. London: Oxford University Press, 1948.

Old Testament. Revised Standard Version. New York: Thomas Nelson & Sons, 1952.

Otto, Walter F. *The Homeric Gods*. Translated by Moses Hadas. New York: Pantheon, 1954.

Pausanias. *Description of Greece*. Translated by W. H. S. Jones. 5 vols. London: William Heinemann, 1918-26.

Perry, Ralph Barton. "The Ego-Centric Predicament," *Journal of Philosophy*, VII (January 6, 1910), 5-14.

———. "A Review of Pragmatism as a Theory of Knowledge," *Journal of Philosophy*, IV (July 4, 1907), 365-74.

———. "A Review of Pragmatism as a Philosophical Generalization," *Journal of Philosophy*, IV (August 1, 1907), 421-28.

———. *The Thought and Character of William James*. 2 vols. London: Oxford University Press, 1935.

Pindar. *The Odes of Pindar*. Translated by John Sandys. London: William Heinemann, 1915.

Plato. *The Dialogues of Plato*. Translated by B. Jowett. 2 vols. New York: Random House, 1937.

Plutarch. *Morals*. Translated by William Baxter and R. Kippox. 4 vols. Boston: Little Brown & Co., 1871.

Pratt, James Bisset. "Truth and Ideas," *Journal of Philosophy*, V (1908), 122-31.

Pringle Pattison, A. Seth. "Review of Studies in Logical Theory," *The Philosophical Review*, XIII (November, 1904), 666-77.

Pritchard, James B., ed. "Ugaritic Myths, Epics, and Legends," *Ancient Near Eastern Texts*. Translated by H. L. Ginsberg. Princeton, New Jersey: Princeton University Press, 1950.

Randall, John Herman, Jr. "Dewey's Interpretation of the History of Philosophy," *The Philosophy of John Dewey*. Edited by Paul Arthur Schilpp. "The Library of Living Philosophers." New York: Tudor Publishing Company, 1951, 77-102.

————. "Dualism in Metaphysics and Practical Philosophy," *Essays in Honor of John Dewey*. New York: Henry Holt and Company, 1929.

————. "Instrumentalism & Mythology," *Journal of Philosophy*, XVI (June 5, 1919), 309-24.

————. "The Really Real," *Journal of Philosophy*, XVII (June 17, 1920), 337-45.

Ratner, Joseph, ed. *John Dewey's Philosophy*. New York: The Modern Library, 1939.

Richardson, Cyril C. *The Doctrine of the Trinity*. New York: Abingdon Press, 1958.

Robinson, Daniel Sommer. "An Alleged New Discovery in Logic," *Journal of Philosophy*, XIV (April 26, 1917), 225-37.

Rogers, A. K. "Professor James's Theory of Knowledge," *The Philosophical Review*, XV (November, 1906), 577-96.

Rohde, Edwin. *Psyche*. Translated by W. B. Hillis. London: Kegan Paul, Trench, Trubner & Co., Ltd., 1925.

Royce, Josiah. "The Eternal & The Practical," *The Philosophical Review*, XIII (March, 1904), 113-42.

————. *William James and Other Essays*. New York: The Macmillan Company, 1911.

Russell, B. "The Basis of Realism," *Journal of Philosophy*, VIII (March 16, 1911), 158-61.

————. "Professor Dewey's Essays in Experimental Logic," *Journal of Philosophy*, XVI (January 2, 1919), 5-26.

Russell, John. "Some Difficulties with the Epistemology of Pragmatism & Radical Empiricism," *The Philosophical Review*, XV (July, 1906), 406-13.

Santayana, George. *Character & Opinion in the United States*. New York: Charles Scribner's Sons, 1920.

————. "Dewey's Naturalistic Metaphysics," *Journal of Philosophy*, XXII (December 3, 1925), 673-88.

————. "Philosophical Heresy," *Journal of Philosophy*, XII (October 14, 1915), 561-68.

————. *The Realm of Matter*. New York: Charles Scribner's Sons, 1930.

————. "Two Rational Moralists," *Journal of Philosophy*, XIII (May 25, 1916), 290-96.

——. *Winds of Doctrine*. London: J. M. Dent & Sons, Ltd., 1913.

Schilpp, Paul Arthur, ed. *The Philosophy of John Dewey*. "The Library of Living Philosophers." New York: Tudor Publisher Company, 1939.

Schinz, Albert. "Professor Dewey's Pragmatism," *Journal of Philosophy*, V (November 5, 1908), 617-28.

Schneider, Herbert W. "Instrumental Instrumentalism," *Journal of Philosophy*, XVIII (March 3, 1921), 113-17.

————. "The Prospect for Empirical Philosophy," *John Dewey, The Man and His Philosophy*. Cambridge: Harvard University Press, 1930, 106-34.

Sellars, R. W. "Professor Dewey's View of Agreement," *Journal of Philosophy*, IV (August 1, 1907), 432-35.

Sheldon, W. H. "Review of Studies in Logical Theory," *Journal of Philosophy*, I (February 18, 1904), 100-05.

―――. "The Vice of Modern Philosophy," *Journal of Philosophy*, XII (January 7, 1915), 5-16.

Spaulding, Edward Gleason. "Joint Discussion with Articles of Agreement and Disagreement: Professor Dewey & Dr. Spaulding," *Journal of Philosophy*, VIII (October 12, 1911), 574-79.

―――. "Realism: A Reply to Professor Dewey & An Exposition," *Journal of Philosophy*, VIII (February 3, 1911), 63-77.

―――. "A Reply to Professor Dewey's Rejoinder," *Journal of Philosophy*, VIII (October 12, 1911), 566-74.

Von Fritz, Kurt. "Greek Prayers," *The Review of Religion* (November, 1945).

Wahl, Jean. *The Pluralist Philosophies of England and America*. London: The Open Court Company, 1925.

White, Morton G. *The Origin of Dewey's Instrumentalism*. New York: Columbia University Press, 1943.

Whitehead, Alfred North. *Adventure of Ideas*. New York: The Macmillan Company, 1933.

Woodbridge, Frederick J. E. "Behavior," *Journal of Philosophy*, XXII (July 16, 1925), 402-11.

―――. *An Essay on Nature*. New York: Columbia University Press, 1940.

―――. "Experience & Dialectic," *Journal of Philosophy*, XXVII (May 8, 1930), 264-71.

―――. *Metaphysics*. New York: The Columbia University Press, 1908.

―――. *Nature and Mind*. New York: The Columbia University Press, 1937.

―――. "Of What Sort Is Cognitive Experience," *Journal of Philosophy*, II (October 12, 1905), 573-76.

―――. "The Problem of Metaphysics," *The Philosophical Review*, XII (July, 1903), 367-85.

―――. "The Promise of Pragmatism," *Journal of Philosophy*, XXVI (September 26, 1929), 541-52.

―――. "Structure," *Journal of Philosophy*, XIV (December 6, 1917), 680-88.

INDEX

Divine, 4
Dogmatism, 2

Egocentric predicament, 121-122
Einstein, 116
El, x, xi, xiii, xiv, 7-12, 28, 29, 30, 33, 34, 73; King, 8; Father of Man, 8; creator, 8; establisher of limits and laws, 10
Eleusinian Mysteries, 13
Empiricism, 2; half hearted, 77, 79; radical, 76, 79, 80, 82, 85, 91, 94, 112
Euclid, 49
Euripides, 19, 23, 25, 163
Evolution, 99

Faith, 95
Fallacy of dogmatism, 53, 57, 58
Fallacy of dualism, 113
Fallacy of fixed ends, 113
Fatalism, 3
Fate, 16
Form, 49, 112, 114, 127, 139, 184; Aristotelian, 56
Free Will, 2, 103-105

Gaster, Theodore, H., discussion of 'punctual' and 'durative' levels, 6, 7
Ginsberg, H. L., 6
God, defined, 10; Father, xi, xiii, 34, 73; Father as transcendent, 30-33; Son, xi, xiii, 34, 73; Son as immanent, 30-33; and nature, 150-151
Greece, ix, xiv; city state, x; paramount concern, x; cultural situation, xi; religion, 4-7, 12-28; myths, 36; Athenians, 49

Habit, 124-127
Hades, 15
Hera, 16
Heracles, 157
Hermes, 29
Herodotus, 19

Hesiod, 16
Hibben, John Grier, 51
Hocking, W. E., 48, 53, 54
Homer, 15, 16, 23, 24, 25, 160
Humboldt, 180
Hume, 77, 78
Hybris, 14, 15, 17
Hypostasis, 30-33

Idealism, 2
Immanent, 7, 10, 20, 22, 29, 34; Baal as, 7-12; Dionysus as, 24, 27; Baal and Dionysus, 26; gods, 73
Ino, 29
Intellectualism, 2
Irrationalism, 94
Irreligion, 3
James, William, xi, xiii, 2, 3, 33, 110, 111, 115, 131, 132, 134, 135, 142, 144, 145, 146, 189; structure in, xiv; criticism of, 34-70; metaphysics of, 71-109; methodological procedure, 36-38

Kant, 77, 78, 115
Kothar, 11

Locke, 78
Lotze, 98
Lovejoy, Arthur O., 47, 48, 60-63, 64, 65, 72, 140, 170, 172
Lycurgus, 24

Magic, 176
Marx, 112
Mary, Mother of God, 32
Materialism, 3
Matter, 49, 112, 199; Aristotelian, 56
McGilvary, E. B., 51, 68
Mill, John Stuart, 98
Mind, 78
Mohammedans, 5
Monism, 2
Montague, W. P., 42, 43, 45, 49, 50, 51, 54, 181
Moore, A. W., 43